ASHE Higher Education Report: Volume 40, Number 2
Kelly Ward, Lisa E. Wolf-Wendel, Series Editors

Community–University Engagement: A Process for Building Democratic Communities

Tami L. Moore

Community–University Engagement: A Process for Building
Democratic Communities
Tami L. Moore
ASHE Higher Education Report: Volume 40, Number 2
Kelly Ward, Lisa E. Wolf-Wendel, Series Editors

Cover image by © Milalala/iStockphoto.

ISSN 1551-6970 electronic   ISSN 1554-6306   ISBN 978-1-118-91745-9

The ASHE Higher Education Report is part of the Jossey-Bass Higher and Adult
Education Series and is published six times a year by Wiley Subscription Services,
Inc., A Wiley Company, at Jossey-Bass, One Montgomery Street, Suite 1200, San
Francisco, California 94104-4594.

Individual subscription rate (in USD): $174 per year US/Can/Mex, $210 rest of
world; institutional subscription rate: $327 US, $387 Can/Mex, $438 rest of world.
Single copy rate: $29. Electronic only–all regions: $174 individual, $327
institutional; Print & Electronic–US: $192 individual, $376 institutional; Print &
Electronic–Canada/Mexico: $192 individual, $436 institutional; Print &
Electronic–Rest of World: $228 individual, $487 institutional. See the Back
Issue/Subscription Order Form in the back of this volume.

CALL FOR PROPOSALS: Prospective authors are strongly encouraged to contact
Kelly Ward (kaward@wsu.edu) or Lisa E. Wolf-Wendel (lwolf@ku.edu). See "About
the ASHE Higher Education Report Series" in the back of this volume.

Visit the Jossey-Bass Web site at **www.josseybass.com.**

The ASHE Higher Education Report is indexed in CIJE: Current Index to
Journals in Education (ERIC), Education Index/Abstracts (H.W. Wilson), ERIC
Database (Education Resources Information Center), Higher Education Abstracts
(Claremont Graduate University), IBR & IBZ: International Bibliographies of
Periodical Literature (K.G. Saur), and Resources in Education (ERIC).

Advisory Board

The ASHE Higher Education Report Series is sponsored by the Association for the Study of Higher Education (ASHE), which provides an editorial advisory board of ASHE members.

Contents

Executive Summary

The interaction between universities and the communities they serve has been a topic of concern for scholars, university administrators, and community leaders since the founding of the earliest colleges in the American colonies during the 17th century. In the 1980s, attention returned to these interactions as communities across the United States experienced urban decay, economic decline, and a variety of related social problems. Thought leaders in higher education and beyond once again positioned colleges and universities as important partners to work with local leaders in addressing the various social, economic, and environmental issues facing communities. This interaction, termed *engagement* by Ernest Boyer (1996) of the Carnegie Foundation, became a very important goal in and of itself, as university leaders worked diligently to position their institutions as engaged in what was considered at the time the very important work of solving social problems and improving the economic well-being of communities. Earning the *engaged* moniker marked an institution, its faculty, and its students as committed to partnering with local communities to address serious community issues.

University presidents and provosts still encourage students, faculty, and administrative professionals to engage with the community today. Students interact with community members through volunteer and community service projects as well as course-based service in community-based agencies providing real-world experience with concepts presented through course materials, termed *service-learning* by teachers and scholars. Faculty members, who have been among the primary actors in the engagement movement, use service-learning in their teaching, and pursue community-engaged research agendas. Administrative professionals represent their university in a wide variety of formal and informal initiatives aimed at advancing cultural and social well-being, and economic development goals.

When university actors interact with communities through different kinds of activities, administrators, faculty, and students operate in ways that implicitly frame community as classroom, laboratory, or locale; each of these frames has material consequences for all members of the community in terms of their access to power and resources. Further, not all interactions between university actors and the surrounding community they inhabit are engaged. This is to say that the term *engagement* connotes specific approaches to relationship building and partnerships. The most widely accepted working definition of engagement emphasizes two values, mutuality and reciprocity. Many higher education institutions provide outreach programs and cultural festivals, such as those detailed in this monograph; these are university programs planned for and delivered to audiences external to the institution without much involvement of community members in determining the goals or approaches to the programming. Research conducted in communities is not necessarily designed or implemented with the input of community members. Community-engaged research is distinguished from community-based research in that the former includes direct involvement of community members in the design and implementation of the research beyond their typical role as participants in or observers of community-based scholarship. Many students provide service to community organizations, such as participating in a Habitat for Humanity home build, without considering the connections between the service and the curriculum of their major field of study. In service-learning, as the saying goes, everyone serves and everyone learns. Community organizations can be partners in the service, and important teachers in the college students' learning process, although they are also sometimes passive recipients of service. Community organizations passively receiving services from students is a characteristic of service, but not of engagement. In contrast, engaged relationships are time and resource intensive to establish and maintain. The culture of community organizations is different than that of higher education institutions. These

instrumental engagement (ie merely "working with" PEII)
vs.)   Critical/Democratic engagement
(C4 p5)PB

and other elements challenge university actors' good intentions, making long-term relationships uncommon in community–university engagement in recent decades, and creating tensions between achieving university goals and living an engagement ethos as a member of the regional community.

To address these issues, higher education actors—administrators, faculty, and students—need to reunderstand the process by which engagement occurs. Each of these constituents must also reconsider the role of communities in community–university engagement. By rethinking these key points, the university actors reevaluate the importance of engaging with all members of the community rather than primarily the well educated and wealthy, and as a result, prioritize a shared vision for community development reflecting the needs and hopes of all residents. Fear, Rosaen, Bawden, and Foster-Fishman (2006) call this new approach "coming to critical engagement" (p. xii). We might also use Saltmarsh and Hartley's (2011) term "democratic engagement" (p. 14) to identify the goal of such a reunderstanding of the values of democratic education: "inclusiveness, participation, task sharing and reciprocity in public problem solving, and an equality of respect for knowledge and experience that everyone involved contributes to education and community building" (p. 17).

Making the shift from instrumental engagement—engaging for the sake of being engaged—to critical, or democratic, engagement is imperative because prioritizing the university's goals continues to marginalize those who are already traditionally underrepresented in conversations about community. One way to move toward democratic engagement is to embrace an engagement ethos that intentionally facilitates broad participation from all demographic groups in discussions about how and in what direction the community should develop in the future, and the resulting initiatives. Through this monograph, I aim to examine this history, call questions that must be answered to continue our commitment to engaging with communities, and finally offer recommendations for doing so.

Foreword

Increasingly, higher education is seen by many as serving a private good (i.e., the beneficiaries of college are those who enroll and graduate). This focus on the private gain of those who attend college has led many state legislatures to decrease public support for higher education and has been credited with the shift from scholarships to loans (the stated logic—if individuals benefit, then why shouldn't they pay?). The balance between whether higher education serves the public or the private good is certainly a topic open to a lot of debate and speculation. But, the two goals don't necessarily have to conflict. Higher education can serve as both a private good and a public good at the same time. Focusing on the role of higher education in contributing to the public good, one can clearly point to the historic and contemporary mission of most colleges and universities. Serving the public, whether that be the local community through town-gown initiatives or the state or regional level or even community defined at the national or international level, is clearly part of the focus and intent of most not-for-profit institutions of higher education. While which community is served varies by institutional type, the idea of serving the public good has long been a goal and focus of many institutions of higher education. How best to meet this goal of serving the public and whether institutions of higher education are going about this in the "right" way is certainly a topic open for debate. Addressing these questions is the focus of this monograph, *Community–University Engagement: A Process for Building Democratic Communities* by Tami L. Moore.

This monograph clearly and succinctly helps the reader to understand how institutions of higher education can best serve the public good. Focusing primarily on the role of research universities, the monograph explores the means by which these institutions serve their communities. For example, sometimes the interaction is through community service projects, sometimes it is through curricular efforts (e.g., service-learning projects), and sometimes it is through research projects. The monograph focuses on the range of who participates in these activities, as some projects are undertaken by students, some by administrative staff, and some by faculty members. In this monograph, Moore explains the difference between working with a community and being truly engaged with the community. The latter is her focus. The monograph artfully articulates how important it is for institutions of higher education to go beyond merely connecting to their communities in order to really serve the public good. The best forms of community interaction, she argues, are reciprocal and call for the community itself to play an active role in the relationship beyond being just the recipient of "help." The monograph explains that to call itself an engaged institution, colleges and universities must work with communities as partners rather than just seeing the community as passive recipients of service. The monograph does an excellent job of explaining the theoretical concepts of engagement and place and reciprocity to better explain to a variety of university constituents how best to be true to the democratic ideals of community engagement. Written for a variety of audiences—from administrators, to faculty members, to policy makers, to community leaders and community members—this monograph articulates a vision for how serving the community could and should look.

The monograph itself represents a solid blend of the prior research literature, pertinent theoretical perspectives as well as concrete examples of community engagement in action. Organized in the format of a traditional research project, the monograph frames a research problem, walks the reader through the relevant literature on various sub-topics relevant to community engagement, and then concludes with suggestions for ways institutions and researchers can learn from this prior literature. The result is a monograph that blends research, theory, and practice into a coherent whole that helps a variety of audiences better understand how institutions of higher education can better fulfill their promise of serving the public good. This monograph is a must read for faculty members who wish to make their research and teaching more relevant to the public, for administrators who oversee community service and service-learning programs, and for community organizers who want to understand why institutions of higher education operate as they do.

Published online in Wiley Online Library
(wileyonlinelibrary.com) • DOI: 10.1002/aehe.20014

[Handwritten annotation at top: "Univ / Community interactions framed [in 3 ways]: 1) emphasizing community & economic development 2) student learning 3) faculty research objectives"]

Overview

T HIS MONOGRAPH EXAMINES the primary ways university faculty, students, and administrators have interacted with the residents and
elected officials of geographic areas where they are located, and the effect of
those interactions on the various participants. The interactions can be framed
in three ways, emphasizing community and economic development, student
learning, or faculty research objectives, respectively. By highlighting each of
these goals/motivations, I am emphasizing the important role that social and
geographically defined place plays in the interactions of universities and the
communities they serve. Institution type matters in the study of higher education in general, because institutional mission and the conditions of operation vary, for example, among research universities, liberal arts colleges, and
community colleges. This monograph focuses on community interaction at
four-year research institutions, and primarily those classified by the Carnegie
Foundation as doctorate-granting universities. The discussion targets administrators who work in colleges and universities, as well as their partners who are
community leaders, elected officials, and staff members in municipal and non-
governmental organizations. To a lesser extent, the monograph also addresses
an audience of scholars and practitioners in higher education administration,
cultural studies in education, cooperative extension, regional studies, urban
and rural planning, K–20 education, community or rural sociology, and geography.

The organization of this monograph replicates, intentionally, the sections
of a research proposal. In the first chapter, I frame a research problem, review
the evolution of the related body of scholarship, and explain the role of place

[Handwritten note in right margin: "centrality of place"]

in community–university engagement as it informs the monograph. Three chapters review the literature related to interaction between community and university. In the second chapter, community is treated as neighborhood, a place where diverse groups of people live and work. The literature reviewed in the third chapter reflects an understanding of community as classroom, where university students connect the college curriculum with the lived experiences of community members. In the fourth chapter, I consider writings about faculty acting as scholars/researchers, working with members of communities conceptualized as laboratory or research context; this body of scholarship includes research findings, as well as discussions about how the engaged institution might evaluate/reward faculty doing engaged scholarship. The third and fourth chapters examine understandings of community as a setting for intellectual activities by faculty and their students. University administrators, faculty, and students are all actors in the region, partnering with others to change conditions within the community. Each of the literature review chapters concludes by highlighting an issue in need of further examination as one moves from thinking of engagement as an outcome in and of itself to understanding engagement as a process for interacting within communities to achieve democratic aims. The fifth chapter reviews the implications of continuing to operationalize community–university engagement as an outcome in and of itself, rather than a process by which university actors engage with community members to realize the civic imperative of higher education. The recommendations highlight possible changes in behavior/practice, as well as empirical research topics holding promise for advancing engagement as a process rather than simply an outcome.

Reframing Engagement

SINCE THE 1980s, NATIONAL LEADERS have been calling for colleges and universities to acknowledge and act upon their civic duty by engaging with the surrounding community. Not only should—the arguments went—the university be developing civic-minded students, but institutional leaders should also more intentionally serve the common good by mobilizing the fiscal, human, and knowledge resources of the institution to address social issues (Bok, 1982; Boyer, 1996; Cantor, 2009; Lynton & Elman, 1987). Pursuant to these new goals, university administrators and professional staff engaged with business and civic leaders to establish community and economic development partnerships. Students participated in academic course-based service, labeled service-learning, and other civic engagement activities including voter education initiatives. Faculty members did their scholarly work in community contexts, and sometimes engaged with community members to carry out research projects.

Several formal definitions of engagement are in common use. Most place heavy emphasis on mutuality and reciprocity, such as this one from the Carnegie Foundation: community–university engagement is "the collaboration between institutions of higher education and their larger communities (local, regional/state, national, global) for the mutually beneficial exchange of knowledge and resources in a context of partnership and reciprocity" (Driscoll, 2008, p. 39). For the purposes of this monograph, engagement is defined simply as "interactions between faculty, students, administrators, or other professional staff members on a given campus and [members of] the geographically-delineated communities primarily located external to the university" (Ward & Moore, 2010, p. 39). This more generic definition acknowledges that not all interactions between university and community representatives currently achieve the mutuality and reciprocity emphasized by other definitions.

Community and educational leaders have encouraged the interaction of community and university across the history of American higher education. Beginning in the 1980s, university leaders renewed their commitment to harnessing institutional resources to address social problems facing local communities. In the 21st century, individual college and university actors participate more intentionally in formal and informal partnerships aimed at advancing economic development and thereby social well-being in a particular community or region. As more and more resources, time, and attention are allocated toward economic development projects such as the rebuilding of New Orleans' Lower Ninth Ward, community development scholars have begun to raise questions about the impact of this approach on community residents (Reardon, Green, Bates, & Kiely, 2009). Too much emphasis on community economic development, or what Bridger and Alter (2006) label "development *in* communities," may have undermined "development *of* communities" (emphasis in original, p. 170). A singular focus on revitalization through economic development will not, the authors argue, necessarily improve the lives of community residents, and may instead shift the decision-making to investors, community developers, and others outside the community (Mathews, 2009; Reardon et al., 2009). Revitalization may actually disenfranchise particular community residents (Barker & Brown, 2009; Bridger & Alter, 2006). To address that possibility, this monograph advances a vision of engagement not as a desired product, but as the necessary process through which the community and university interact to strengthen communities at the local and regional level.

Engagement as a process, as it is conceptualized in this monograph, matches Fear, Rosaen, Bawden and Foster-Fishman's (2006) definition of critical engagement: "opportunities to share . . . knowledge and learn with [all] those who struggle for social justice; and to collaborate . . . respectfully and responsibly for the purpose of improving life" (p. xiii). Fear et al.

differentiate critical engagement from instrumental engagement, which focuses narrowly on completing specific tasks and projects. Engagement-as-process, like critical engagement, is a transformative experience for all involved: "The primary value is the effect it has on participants, helping them think intentionally and deeply about themselves, their work, and how they approach their practice" (p. 257). It is in this sense that I link engagement-as-process to Fear et al.'s definition of critical engagement as a transformative learning and community-building endeavor including diverse members of a geographically specific community.

The Emergence of a Field of Study

Engagement-as-process as defined in this monograph emerges from the scholarly discussion of the interaction of communities and universities as it has developed over three decades through six discernible, but not distinct, approaches to issues related to engagement taken by scholars and practitioners: defining engagement, documenting and describing engagement, advancing engagement as scholarship, institutionalizing engagement, considering community experiences with engagement, and engaging for democracy. These approaches reflect overlapping trends in peer-reviewed scholarship, scholarly books and position papers written by professional/disciplinary associations, independent gatherings of scholars and practitioners. The following discussion addresses each of these individually, moving from the early writing focused on defining, documenting, and describing engagement to institutional issues such as rewarding faculty for engaged scholarly work, before turning to consider the effect of engagement on communities, and the reemerging discourse linking engagement and democracy.

Defining Engagement

National reports, such as the Kellogg Commission on the Future of State and Land-Grant Universities' (1999) *Returning to Our Roots: Executive Summaries of the Reports of the Kellogg Commission on the Future of State and Land-Grant Universities*, called for a "return" or a "renewal" of what many leaders in the

---

1980s and 1990s framed as the historic commitment of American higher education institutions to civic purposes and the public good. Higher education leaders, in turn, asked faculty and administrators to expand traditional concepts of university outreach to emphasize mutuality and reciprocity. Early writing on engagement served two purposes: defining the characteristics of specific varieties of engagement (i.e., service-learning and community partnerships); and making the case to other administrators and faculty based on community needs and the expectations of funders, including state legislatures (Sandmann, 2008). Early service-learning scholarship sought to distinguish teaching practices linking course material to service with community entities to reinforce desired learning from a wide variety of community-based experiential learning activities (Stanton, 1987). Definitions of engagement published during this period, such as Furco's (1996) typology of community-based learning activities, emphasized mutual benefit to both learner and recipient as a defining characteristic of service-learning, differentiating it from the broader category of experiential learning (Kendall, 1990).

Documenting/Describing Engagement

Beginning in the mid-1990s, authors offered detailed descriptions of service-learning and community partnerships to differentiate engagement from public service and outreach. The case studies emphasized benefits for university and community, embodying mutuality and reciprocity (e.g., O'Brien & Accardo, 1996). Even so, very few authors gave attention to public participation in knowledge generation, indicating that the distinction between one-way outreach by university knowledge experts and two-way cocreation of knowledge through engagement remained relatively nascent in this stage (Glass & Fitzgerald, 2010; Sandmann, 2008).

Advancing Engagement as Faculty Work

Fairweather (1996) insisted on the need to align promotion and tenure guidelines and other elements of faculty reward systems with the increased emphasis on civic values as the most expedient way to realize institutional goals for engagement. The peer-reviewed literature published after the late 1990s reflects this shift, as more manuscripts reporting findings from community-engaged

6

research appeared, along with pieces advocating community-based and participatory methodologies (Minkler & Wallerstein, 2003; Sandmann, 2008). By 2000, two paradigms existed in the literature, reflecting two separate bodies of theory and practice related to community engagement: institutional civic engagement or the work of administrators to establish partnerships resulting in community revitalization on varying scales, and community-engaged scholarship enacted by faculty as scholar–researchers (Sandmann, 2008; see also Glass & Fitzgerald, 2010; Hodges & Dubb, 2012).

Institutionalizing Engagement

As the faculty work discussion expanded, engagement scholars began to grapple with the tensions between the traditional expertise-driven culture of the academy and the new epistemology of the civic engagement movement (Butin, 2003, 2006; O'Meara, 2010; Schön, 1995). A rich body of literature developed, outlining promising practices and addressing the role of institutional culture in this work (e.g., Hyman et al., 2001/2002; O'Meara & Rice, 2005). Scholars who study the process of engagement also began to draw on organizational theory to examine issues related to organizational behavior (e.g., Kezar, 2011; Van de Ven, 2007; Weerts & Sandmann, 2008, 2010). Work continues to appear in this area as institutional leaders and scholar–practitioners advance engagement as an institutional priority.

Considering Community in Engagement Activities

Engagement, by definition, focused on community problems, so even the earliest works alluded to the role of the community at least as the location of engagement (Boyer, 1996). Nonetheless, a greater emphasis on the impact of engagement on communities, as well as the involvement of community members in the planning of engagement initiatives, emerged slowly. Notable contributions in this area highlight community partner perspectives; offer evaluations of existing community partnerships, as well as standards for such evaluation; and discuss characteristics of effective partnerships (Anyon & Fernández, 2007; Israel et al., 2006; McNall, Reed, Brown, & Allen, 2009; Nye & Schramm, 1999; Sandy & Holland, 2006; Stoecker, Beckman, & Min, 2010; Vidal, Nye, Walker, Manjarrez, & Romanik, 2002). Much of the

---

scholarship and practice of community–university engagement continues to overlook community outcomes and the specific experiences of community leaders partnering with universities (Reardon et al., 2009; Sandy & Holland, 2006; Stoecker & Tryon, 2009; Stoecker et al., 2010).

Engaging for Democracy

q4b

The early scholarship on community–university engagement, particularly related to service-learning, reflected a sustained debate on the role of civic engagement, for students as well as for institutions. By the mid-1990s, two primary objectives were discernible in the discussion of desired student learning outcomes: advancing social change/democratic ideals and supporting discipline-specific learning outcomes (Saltmarsh & Zlotkowski, 2011). Around 2008, civic engagement scholars revived this debate, calling for democratic engagement, and renewed emphasis on higher education's historical role of educating for citizenship and civic/political leadership (Barker & Brown, 2009; Saltmarsh & Hartley, 2011).

Each of the six approaches summarized in this section represents one way to focus a conversation that is wide-ranging and difficult to navigate. Placing too much emphasis on any of the individual approaches has tended to distract scholars and practitioners from the potential for community–university engagement to transform universities as well the communities they serve. Such transformative change is necessary because the current structure of the university and the culture of individual institutions present barriers to realizing the potential of institutional actors to partner with community members and foster real change in communities affected by social issues and the ups and downs of the U.S. economy.

Using Theory to Advance Community–University Engagement

The engagement literature includes many examples of scholars utilizing theoretical constructs to explore interactions between community and university *theory:*

actors. Theories explain why things work the way they do, and suggest "how things . . . might work differently" in a particular setting or within a given problem (Nealon & Giroux, 2003, p. 4). A theoretical framework is like a picture frame. The frame "guides your [attention] to the image inside the frame instead of what surrounds it" and plays an important role in shaping research design, "help[ing] us to focus on one set of interesting and important questions about a particular topic" (Jaeger et al., 2013, p. 13).

Employing organizational theory, many authors have examined relationships among individual actors, as well as the interactions of the organizations—university, community-based entities, and the partnership itself—with each other and their environments. Community development scholar-practitioners, although very rarely represented in the scholarship related to engagement, have also offered models to theorize community engagement (Bortolin, 2011; Stoecker et al., 2010). Full discussion of the rich literature related to each of these theoretical traditions is outside the scope of this work. Instead, I offer a brief overview of studies employing organizational theory and community development models, as examples of questions previously explored using these constructs.

Organizational Theory

Examining engagement as organizational behavior allows scholars to consider questions related to institutional policies and practices. Each of these elements can enable or frustrate administrator and faculty efforts to deepen interactions between universities and communities; organizational theories provide tools for explaining those challenges and suggesting new ways forward. Findings from studies informed by organizational theories provide useful insights as to the way in which individual representatives, and the organization as a whole, change in the process of adopting an engagement ethos (Holland, 2009). Over three decades, we have learned a great deal about what supports engagement.

Achieving the ideal of reciprocal community–university engagement requires a willingness to transcend traditional boundaries and, in some instances, create new ones. Reciprocity is fostered in these relationships by

Reciprocity

information sharing that goes both ways, moving away from the traditional university outreach model (Weerts & Sandmann, 2008). Embracing engagement as a process will include community and university representatives making a commitment to two-way knowledge flow. This innovation will not happen until "environmental change makes existing boundaries unworkable, when the organizational fails to achieve desired goals, or when it is thought that goals can be better satisfied in another manner" (Levine, 1980, as cited by Sandmann & Weerts, 2008, p. 183). University leaders must come to understand that the current approach to engagement as outcome has made firm boundaries between universities and communities unworkable, thereby threatening the university's ability to achieve its desired goals. Universities may have missions that are compatible with engagement and simultaneously exhibit cultural values and norms that present barriers to engagement. Understanding how shifts in structure and culture affect engagement and the ultimate sustainability of the initiatives will also be vital to smoothing the transition from outcome- to process-oriented engagement. Boundary spanners, adept at translating cultural norms and values and coaching administrators into a new way of partnering, will also be critical to the success of these changes (Miller, 2008; Weerts & Sandmann, 2010).

The value of organizational theories employed in research about community–university engagement lies in their usefulness for highlighting the elements of organizations that influence institutional ability to pursue engagement (Weerts & Sandmann, 2008, pp. 81–83). The difference between the organizational cultures of universities and community organizations merits further consideration as well, given that these differences undermine many partnerships (Kezar, 2011). What organizational theories do not offer is necessary insight into the community dynamics that contextualize all engagement initiatives. Community development models fill this gap.

Community and Economic Development Models
Community development scholar–practitioners focus on the development of community infrastructure to support instrumental development activities such as business creation and infrastructure development. Universities

are often implicit actors in these models. Keane and Allison (1999) argue that "[t]he value of higher education" in the global economy "lies in the linkages and quality of [universities'] embeddedness in the local economy" (p. 896). By embeddedness, the authors mean something like the degree to which university actors contribute to what Flora and Flora (1993) call *entrepreneurial social infrastructure* (ESI). A community's ESI reflects a network of civic and business leaders mobilizing human, fiscal, and physical resources to promote local development and sustain connections with other similarly situated communities. University administrators are important partners in these activities because of their ability to leverage institutional resources to strengthen community infrastructure (Sharp, Flora, & Killacky, 2003).

Higher education scholars and practitioners are not, however, well versed in this literature (Stoecker et al., 2010). Rather than viewing community as a place where engagement takes place, university actors typically position community as a place to advance university objectives (Bortolin, 2011). Community developers instead consider the process of interacting as equally as important as the outcome of the interactions. The community development literature best serves community–university engagement when the models prioritize economic and community well-being over university interests because higher education institutions located in strong communities benefit from that vitality.

The Role of Place in Engagement

By calling attention to when and how theory has been used in the scholarship of engagement, I am intentionally emphasizing the contributions that sophisticated and rich conceptual models have made to scholars' and practitioners' understanding of when, how, and to what end engagement has been or can be employed. This monograph draws explicitly on critical geography. The guiding questions consider how differing conceptualizations of community influence the interactions between community and university actors, and also how those conceptualizations inform the structure and outcomes of community–university interaction.

Community–university interactions are place-based in that they usually occur in a specific geographic location (Moore, 2013). Labeling an interaction as place-based is another way of saying the history, culture, and socioeconomics of a physical location, as well as the interactions of people in that place, should be noted as very important details when examining interactions between university actors and the communities they serve. Critical geographers explore indicators of social, cultural, and economic power and how people who possess power in a particular community shape the places where they live and work (Cresswell, 2004).

Giving closer consideration to the way university actors think about the places where engagement initiatives occur invites us to examine the power university actors wield and also how they use this power to influence change in a community. When we ask questions about power and how it is used in the context of engagement, we learn what university actors believe about what could or should be done in that place/community, who could or should be involved in the partnerships, and the primary beneficiaries of these activities. Knowing what and how actors think is important in moving toward engagement-as-process. How engagement leaders conceptualize community impacts not only the outcomes of particular initiatives but also the socioeconomic well-being and social relations among people living in that place.

Place, for critical geographers, is a social construct, meaning that a particular physical or virtual location has no inherently uniform meaning or value. The meaning or value assigned to various characteristics of the place or community has been negotiated through the interaction of residents and visitors alike (Kyle & Chick, 2007). This is true of physical places: universities are widely understood to be sites of expert knowledge, while communities have been situated as the recipients of that knowledge, inherently lacking expertise. Human interaction also invests social place with meaning; in this case, place refers to social status or social location within a group of relationships. Those who have not earned a university degree, for example, are often understood to be and therefore treated as less expert than graduates, especially advanced degree holders such as university faculty and administrators. Critical

Critical Geographers

geographers, on the other hand, recognize community members as powerful knowledge resources (Keith & Pile, 1993).

How participants in a given engagement initiative think about a particular community and its residents has political consequences, in that the social construction of that place may determine how much access particular members of the community have to power structures and/or material resources. When we examine a partnership, we can learn about access to power by asking questions about who determined the goals of the program, how those goals were determined, and who benefits from the program. A university located contiguously to a low-income neighborhood might possess greater economic resources and social influence than the surrounding community, and may be perceived as having greater intellectual resources than local residents (Maurrasse, 2001). The relative assessment of the neighborhood's intellectual resources is itself influenced by the larger society's read on the relative value or social influence of a college degree versus lived experience. The way we talk about or otherwise depict a place can also have "material consequences" (Harvey, 1993, p. 22). If, for example, community members are conceptualized as participants in a research project, rather than members of the research team, funding for the study may be paid exclusively to the university rather than reimbursing the community members for time contributed to the research project. adh '.

Discussing the way in which places are conceptualized by those who inhabit them acknowledges that how people think about or conceptualize communities influences the objectives that will be pursued through those relationships and hence the way in which university and community partners behave in those places, with whom they do or do not build relationships, and how power is shared among the participants. The process by which university actors identify community leaders/possible engagement partners likely takes into consideration, consciously or not, the educational attainment, socioeconomic class, gender, race/ethnicity, and cultural capital of specific individuals; as a result, individuals in traditionally underrepresented groups are also in many cases underrepresented in engagement initiative leadership roles.

Place, and the way people invest themselves in that place, shapes the terms of engagement: who participates, who sets the agenda, and to what end the partnership is pursued. For this reason, I give attention in the following chapters to how community is conceptualized, or framed, when the conversation turns to a particular variety of community–university interactions. The interactions have been framed by scholars and practitioners in three ways, understanding community as neighborhood, as classroom, and as research context, and prioritizing community economic development, student learning, and faculty scholarship, respectively. Each frame offers a different way of understanding the relationships between university and community actors and suggests ways to address issues facing individual partnerships, and the engagement movement as a whole.

A Roadmap

The interactions of university faculty, students, and administrators at institutions classified by the Carnegie Foundation as doctorate-granting universities with the residents and elected officials of the local region, and the effect of those interactions on the various participants can be framed in three ways, as outlined above. The frames reflect the goals of university actors, emphasizing community and economic development, student learning, or faculty research objectives, respectively. This monograph follows the organizational scheme used in a social science research proposal to examine the important role that socially and geographically defined place plays in the interactions between universities and the communities they serve. This chapter has framed a research problem, reviewed the evolution of the related body of scholarship, demonstrated the use of theory in research design, and offered a theoretical frame for this monograph by querying the role of place in community–university engagement. Place as a social construct is operationalized in an a priori fashion in this monograph, in the sense that I begin with and proceed from my conviction that community–university engagement is inherently place-based, reflecting the history, culture, and socioeconomics of the community, and must be studied this way if we are to understand these interactions in a way that advances democratic processes (Moore, 2013).

Chapter review/goals

The next three chapters review the literature related to three different types of interactions between community and university. In the second chapter, community is treated as neighborhood, or place where diverse groups of people live, work, and partner with others to change conditions within the community. The third and fourth chapters examine understandings of community as a setting for intellectual activities by faculty as teachers and their students, and then faculty as researchers. Each of these chapters concludes by highlighting an issue in need of further examination as one moves from thinking of engagement as an outcome in and of itself to understanding engagement as a process for interacting within communities to achieve democratic aims. The fifth chapter reviews the implications of continuing to operationalize community–university engagement as an outcome, and concludes by offering recommended changes in behavior/practice, as well as empirical research topics holding promise for advancing engagement as a process rather than an outcome.

Community – university Partnership

Acts of Placemaking ⟩ re the practice of democracy

3-part phenomenon :

in order to have strong Community-University Partnerships, institutions must make [Engagement] central to the Mission

the university as actor in the broad Community

placemaker": an org actively shaping character of the Community

Community as Place

COMMUNITY–UNIVERSITY ENGAGEMENT is inherently place-based in the sense that interactions such as those described in this monograph happen in a particular locale. Universities contribute to the social and cultural milieu of the places where they are located in three primary ways: as educator, preparing students for active citizenship and future employment; as information resource for addressing community issues; and as partner in formal community and economic development initiatives. In order to have strong community–university partnerships, institutions must make engagement central to their mission. Colleges and universities have done this in many different ways, as befits the places where they are located. This chapter focuses on the work of higher education institutions to provide arts/cultural programming and other services for local residents and to strengthen community infrastructures. A discussion of the university as an actor in the broad community opens the monograph because the examples presented in this chapter represent the prevailing understanding of community and university leaders alike about the role of higher education institutions in communities. These attitudes underlie much of the current thinking about when, how, with whom, and to what end university representatives should engage with community members.

In this chapter, I highlight three ways that universities have pursued these goals: as placemaker, as economic development partner, and more recently by enacting an anchor institution mission. Each term reflects a particular set of ideas from the literature on community–university engagement. I use the term *placemaker* in this chapter to connote an entity actively shaping the

---

character of the communities it serves through activities such as those outlined in the following section (Schneekloth & Shibley, 1995). When university administrators/agents act as community development partners in a community or region, they harness institutional resources to support the generation of new jobs, new technologies, and new industries in local communities. Very recently, universities have begun to recognize their importance as an anchor institution in a particular community; scholar–practitioners and policy makers use the term *anchor institution* to emphasize the ways in which universities are anchored to the places where they are located. Unlike corporations, higher education institutions would be unlikely if not unable to relocate in search of, for example, more attractive tax incentives. As an anchor institution, the university plays a key role in the social and economic well-being of a community. Institutional leaders can be said to be enacting an anchor institution mission when they recognize the role of their university in the place where it is located, and then proactively contribute to stronger local economies and increase individual and collective well-being (Hodges & Dubb, 2012).

Each of these roles reflects the scholarly discussion of community–university engagement as well as various aspects of the argument I am advancing in this monograph. By insisting on locating these interactions in a particular city or region, I am also intentionally highlighting the importance of "all the particulars of nature and culture that locally shape human perception of, and participation in" that place (Fettes & Judson, 2011, p. 123). Formal partnerships and informal interactions alike can serve either or both of these purposes. This chapter reviews examples of each, and examines the literature related to community–university partnerships, shifting ideas about the role of higher education in community development efforts, and the emerging anchor institution movement, featuring institutions as diverse as LeMoyne-Owen College and Yale University, and the community development partnerships institutional leaders are forming with community organizations. Examples of placemaking, community–university partnerships, and activities reflecting an anchor institution mission follow in this chapter; each represents a different focus for university activities in geographically or socially defined communities.

3 element of Placemaking 1) what is done in a place?
2) How it is done?
3) underlying values

Placemaking — *as a practice of democracy*

Higher education institutions are key partners in placemaking, the process by which human beings "transform the places in which we find ourselves into places in which we live" (Schneekloth & Shibley, 1995, p. 1; see also Herts, 2011). The work of placemaking is "poetic," rather than "technical" or instrumental, because "the making of places—our homes, our neighborhoods, our places of work and play—not only changes and maintains the physical world of living; it also is a way we make our communities and connect with other people" (Schneekloth & Shibley, 1995, pp. 1–2). Scholars who frame community–university interaction as placemaking ask questions about what is done in a place, how it is done, and the values that underlie those activities. Understanding these three elements of the placemaking process provides important background information supporting efforts to change some part of a community or a group's story. Acts of placemaking are not just about "strengthening relationships of people to their places" through, for example, festivals celebrating local history. The placemaking process also creates public spaces, through neighborhood planning initiatives or other municipal processes, and "foster[s]. . . relationships *among* the people in places" that support community infrastructures (emphasis in original; Schneekloth & Shibley, 1995, p. 1). Placemaking is, in this way, "the practice of democracy" (Schneekloth & Shibley, 1995, p. 110). University representatives can support cities in engaging citizens in civil dialogue. For example, municipal officials and community members in Roanoke, Virginia, consulted with urban planning scholar–practitioners from a local university, requesting assistance in restructuring the functionality of the Roanoke Neighborhood Partnership (RNP) and the City of Roanoke's Office of Community Planning; the aim was to make it easier for residents to make their neighborhoods better, and to do so in a community-driven way. City officials faced specific challenges: several decades of urban decay, reduced federal spending on community revitalization, and fiscal austerity. These officials saw residents and neighborhood associations as important and very willing participants in neighborhood revitalization projects. The problem, the new mayor realized, was a city government structure that did

---

not facilitate public participation. The RNP hosted a series of community planning sessions facilitated by the consultants; with the assistance of university scholar–practitioners, residents designed an easy-to-navigate process facilitating the participation of interested citizens, thereby advancing democratic practices in the city.

Places are also made through formal, intentional collaborative efforts involving senior university officials and requiring the dedication of institutional resources and, in some cases, significant change in the way the institution operates. Arizona State University's downtown campus provides one such example. Around 2006, ASU officials joined Phoenix leaders in imagining a new arrangement for the downtown area (Fettes & Judson, 2011). Over the next three years, the university contributed to realizing that vision by constructing a downtown campus, establishing a new College of Public Programs to be housed there, and relocated other academic units whose mission fit that of an urban campus (Friedman, 2009). The RNP and ASU's downtown campus represent small- and large-scale, informal and formal partnerships that strengthen relationships of people to the places where they live and among those people who live there.

Schneekloth and Shibley (1995) explain placemaking as a three-part phenomenon: changing the physical place, strengthening the relationships of people to that place, and enhancing interpersonal relationships. Formal and informal partnerships and programming ranging from cultural events bringing visitors to the community, to continuing education offerings and university extension and outreach programs each constitute placemaking. Examples of each type of placemaking are offered in the following sections.

Community Tourism

Higher education institutions are important partners in regional tourism development (Herts, 2011). Increasingly, campuses house visitor centers. Many such centers were opened by an Office of Admissions to greet prospective students and their families. Through partnerships with state convention and visitors' bureaus or departments of tourism, several of these have been recognized as official state visitor centers. Visitors attend athletic and cultural events, arts and music festivals, and other community-based activities.

For example, the University of Idaho hosts the Lionel Hampton Jazz Festival each February; in 2007, the National Endowment for the Arts recognized the event with the National Medal of Arts, the nation's most prestigious arts award. Each year, more than 8000 tickets are sold for concerts, master classes, lectures, and other performances by world-class musicians. Middle and high school choirs and jazz bands from across the Pacific Northwest travel to Moscow, Idaho, for solo and ensemble competitions during the festival, and the Jazz in the Schools program connects nearly 8000 students from K–12 schools in the surrounding area with visiting musicians. Community residents participate in smaller arts festivals at other universities: Auburn University's Tournees Film Festival invites community members to campus for French cinema; the Ohio State University's MFA Alumni Bookfair and Festival offers book readings/signings and public lectures on creative writing and small press publishing.

Continuing Education

Film festivals and cultural events represent lifelong learning opportunities. Cantor (2006) links lifelong learning with professional continuing education, describing a multifaceted endeavor. These various activities extend the placemaking efforts/capacity of universities in a variety of ways. Very commonly, universities act as workforce development partners by offering certificate programs and continuing education courses required in various professions (e.g., nursing, veterinary medicine, and counseling) to working professionals through university continuing education units. The wide range of activities offered by the University of Georgia are typical of many U.S. institutions. The Georgia Center, the university's conference facility, hosts thousands of guests each year, including fans attending university athletics events, conference attendees, and participants in short-term industry-specific professional development courses. Community groups such as the Georgia Hospice Palliative Care Organization, state high school sports officials, and the Georgia Water Resources Board have recently chosen the Georgia Center for their conferences, making this professional development center a key resource for the state's professional community.

Cont Education serve "free agent learners"

Elderhostel Continuing education units also serve *free agent learners* (Caudron, 2004) who pursue continuing education to achieve personal development goals. These lifelong learners resemble the original patrons of programs like Elderhostel, providing residential short courses for older learners since 1976 (and today operating as Road Scholar, www.roadscholar.org), and Osher Lifelong Learning Institute programs on campuses across the United States. See, for example, the University of Delaware's tuition-free degree completion program for Delaware residents over 60 (http://www.pcs.udel.edu/credit/over60.html).

Connectors Continuing education professionals are also important participants in
Conveners community/university interactions intended to serve the public good (Shannon & Wang, 2010). Continuing education units "are in a unique position to build connections . . . across both campus and community," and thereby "accelerat[e] connectedness with the greater community" (p. 109). They act as conveners, linking academic faculty with community members/organizations to address specific issues, such as community emergency response and professional development for nonprofit organizations, and thereby transform the communities served by these groups.

University Extension

Lifelong learning opportunities for personal and professional enhancement are also available through university extension programs. The Smith-Lever Act of 1914 established the national cooperative extension system, comprised of extension units at each of the 50 land-grant universities established under the Morrill Act of 1862. Extension professionals are employed by the university and placed in every county in each state to provide programming and services to the residents of that county. The traditional image of a county extension agent depicts an agriculture expert focused on "cows, plows, and sows" (D. Barton, personal communication, January 15, 2001), educating farmers and ranchers on topics related to crop management and animal husbandry. Historically, Family Consumer Science (formerly Home Economics) agents organized demonstration clubs focused on traditional household management and child rearing activities, and facilitated friendship networks for isolated rural women who worked at home (Allen, Dunn, & Zaslow, 2011). Neither of these descriptions reflects 21st century extension professionals, who are actively involved in community economic development, and programming targeted toward improving the quality of life for young people, families, and other residents in communities of every size across the United States (McDowell, 2001).

The issues addressed by extension professionals differ from state to state and, as a result, so does the variety of organizations/agencies in their network (e.g., faith-based organizations, public schools, trade associations, social service organizations, community/cultural organizations, state government, private associations, and professional associations; Bartholomay, Chazdon, Marczak, & Walker, 2011). The extent of the networks, as well as the importance of these networks to extension programming and partnerships, would however be virtually the same across the United States. For example, the University of Minnesota Extension's organizational network is very wide, and includes several sub-networks clustered around particular program areas (Bartholomay et al., 2011). The network is maintained through five types of relationships: contributing administrative, financial, or physical labor support (7.5%); providing substantive information (22.4%); offering expert advice (15.7%); influencing an organization's processes/outcomes (11.3%); and sustaining formal partnerships (43.1%). In other words, slightly under half of the University of Minnesota's network relationships are focused on formal partnerships structured "around a joint effort with mutual benefit" (Bartholomay et al., 2011, Figure 1). This final statistic suggests that extension professionals are not only an important part of the land-grant university's outreach effort, but also key contributors to the university's community engagement initiatives and to placemaking.

University extension contributes to placemaking by developing the capacity of individuals and community organizations to accomplish goals together (Civittolo & Davis, 2011). Extension professionals play an important role in building and supporting social networks linking university actors with community organizations and individual residents. The relationships that underlie these networks facilitate identifying issues, exploring possible options to address the issues, building community support for proposed solutions or programming, and establishing mutually beneficial, reciprocal partnerships (Adedokun & Balschweid, 2009; Robinson & Meikle-Yaw, 2007).

Community–University Partnerships

Community well-being in many U.S. metropolitan areas seems bleak after several decades of de-industrialization, suburbanization, and shifting federal funding priorities. Today, the U.S. urban landscape is changing under the influence of shifting federal funding priorities and philosophies of government intervention in individuals' lives. Community officials and nonprofit sector leaders all over the United States turn to university actors when seeking partners for revitalization projects, or in an effort to grow new opportunities supporting a community's prosperity (Dubb & Howard, 2007; Hodges & Dubb, 2012).

Community–university partnerships have a long history in the United States, dating to the 19th century settlement houses. For example, Jane Addams partnered with faculty at the University of Chicago; UC students regularly volunteered at Hull House (Hodges & Dubb, 2012, pp. 3–6). Established partnerships now exist in cities across the United States, and the literature related to effective partnership practices is broad, spanning many disciplines (e.g., Hartley & Soo, 2009; Israel et al., 2006; McNall et al., 2009; Prigge & Torraco, 2007). Two of the longest running partnerships exist in East St. Louis, Illinois, and West Philadelphia, Pennsylvania.

East St. Louis. In 1987, a group of ministers from the poorest neighborhoods of East St. Louis, Illinois, contacted their state representative requesting assistance in establishing a partnership with the University of Illinois to address chronic issues facing their community. The resulting partnership, the East St. Louis Action Research Project (ESLARP), continued for 23 years, making it one of the longest running, formal community–university partnerships in the United States (Reardon, 1999; Sorenson & Lawson, 2011). Over more than two decades, the relationship evolved from a one-way outreach/professional expert model into a participatory action research project, primarily involving faculty and students in UIUC's Department of Urban and Regional Planning, and community leaders and elected officials. One notable success: "a new mixed-use, mixed-income, mixed-finance [housing] development in the area surrounding the newly built Emerson Park Rail Station" (Reardon, 2003, "Parsons Place," para. 2). This project, like so many other successes in the ESLARP partnership, did not originate with university representatives or elected officials. Instead, a community member empowered to speak for the community and supported by university faculty negotiated with the power structures which have traditionally constrained community options for self-directed economic and community development successes in East St. Louis. This community-driven agenda setting, drawing on the university for support, was characteristic of the partnership for most of its history, making ESLARP a striking example of engagement as a process to engage a broad representation of community in the partnership activities.

West Philadelphia. One of the earliest community–university partnerships still in existence links the neighborhoods of West Philadelphia with the University of Pennsylvania, and provides another example of the engagement-as-process ethos advanced in this monograph. The community–university relationship between "West Philly," as the residents call their home, and Penn has matured significantly over the last three decades (Benson & Harkavy, 2000). The West Philadelphia Improvement Corps (WEPIC) began in 1985 as an after-school program at a local elementary school; WEPIC has grown over three decades to include educational collaborations, urban clean-up projects, and environmental stewardship efforts between Penn faculty and students, parents, and community members at various K–12 schools in West Philadelphia (Benson, Harkavy, & Puckett, 1996, 2000).

Today, the Barbara and Edward Netter Center for Community Partnerships is Penn's main vehicle for these programs. The Center supports more than a dozen other diverse collaborations, ranging from improving college access to redesigning local business models. The Netter Center at Penn strives to solve the complex, comprehensive, and interconnected problems of local urban living through mutually beneficial and respectful partnerships with the West Philadelphia community (Netter Center, 2012).

Support for Other Partnerships. Financial as well as philosophical support for community–university partnerships is evident on many fronts, including universities, philanthropic foundations, state and local governments, and national policy organizations, such as Campus

Compact, a coalition of 1100 university presidents and the institutions they lead committed to furthering the civic mission of higher education. Marga, Inc.—a consulting firm headed by scholar–practitioner David Maurrasse—and the members of the national Anchor Institution Task Force (http://www.margainc.com/initiatives/aitf/) engage with universities and their communities to build capacity for collaborative partnerships recognizing the university as a key player in the economic stability and growth of the United States' cities. Other organizations, such as CEOs for Cities, recognize higher education's important role in economic development, building on the work of Florida (2004, 2005) who has long advocated the importance of higher education in attracting creative entrepreneurial professionals to a community as the cornerstone of urban growth. The Talloires Network, an international coalition of universities in 71 countries committed to engagement, the Association of Public and Land-Grant Universities, and the Kellogg Foundation are among the many organizations that recognize excellence in community–university partnership with annual awards and cash prizes.

The many examples of placemaking activities presented above indicate that universities around the United States are actively responding to calls by civic and education leaders to engage with their communities. Most community members, and many senior university leaders, focus on high visibility formal partnerships such as these as the venue for acting on calls for engagement. Some partnerships do show evidence of broad-based community participation in the planning process, but others do not. Even so, all could be said to advance the university's goal for engagement. The examples offered in this chapter reflect intentional partnerships, and—in some instances—community leadership in setting the agenda for the partnership. However, many other institutions still emphasize engagement as a product rather than shifting to an engagement ethos as a way to facilitate broad participation to advance the community's vision for itself. *NB.*

Driving the Economy

The Great Recession of 2008–2010 brought a new urgency to discussions of community–university interaction. Business/civic leaders, senior university administrators, and higher education scholars now use terms like *economic driver* to describe the role of universities in economic development (Lane & Johnstone, 2012). This rhetoric is particularly common from civic and business leaders. More than a decade ago, higher education scholar Alexander (2000) characterized this economic engine role as "an increasing burden on higher education" (p. 412). Others worried publicly that the commercialization of research was threatening the free exchange of ideas upon which academia depends (Williams-Jones, 2005). Nonetheless, there were also examples of university leaders advocating institutional involvement, and sometimes outright leadership, in economic development particularly at metropolitan universities (O'Brien & Accardo, 1996; O'Brien, Grace, Williams, Paradise, & Gibbs, 2003). Today, high profile leaders such as State University of New York Chancellor Nancy Zimpher embrace the economic engine role enthusiastically: "[T]he path to [U.S.] economic vitality . . .is ahead of us," she has suggested, and ". . . America's universities, colleges, and community colleges will build the bridge to get us there" (USC Rossier School of Education, 2013).

Faculty and administrators promote economic vitality in multiple ways (Lane, 2012). Through multisector collaborations, universities create research infrastructures with an eye to establishing an industrial cluster in a particular region (Shaffer & Wright, 2010). For example, the Georgia Research Alliance hosts the Eminent Scholars initiative. With matching funds from state and university partners, Eminent Scholars has attracted 60 scholar–entrepreneurs to the Atlanta area, brought in $2.6 billion in research funding, generated 150 new companies, and created 5500 jobs in the science and technology fields. Universities support local businesses through workforce development initiatives, small business development services, and entrepreneurship training. The Riata Center for Entrepreneurship Studies at Oklahoma State University in Tulsa offers similar experiences through a six-week "Entrepreneur Boot Camp" for micro- and small businesses in Northeast Oklahoma. Higher education institutions also prepare their graduates as new members of the workforce educated for the knowledge economy and socialized to engage in the civic life of their communities (Johnstone, 2012).

Higher education institutions are also "spender[s] and consumer[s]," acting as "economic units" in their local community (Gais & Wright, 2012, p. 34). Universities receive revenue in the form of tuition and research grant dollars, which is in turn spent on employee salaries, utility costs, office supplies, and materials for use in construction projects. Students and their occasionally visiting parents, alumni, and university employees contribute directly to the local economy, through expenditures on living expenses, travel, lodging, dining, and entertainment. Universities themselves are also important customers of local businesses. For example, in 2008–2009, the overall economic impact of the University of Iowa on the state was $6.0 billion; this figure includes $2.6 billion in direct expenditures, and an additional $3.4 billion in "induced or indirect spending within the state" (Tripp Umbach, 2010, p. 1); in short, "[e]ach $1 invested in the University of Iowa [through state funding, for example] returns $15.81 to the state" in revenue (Tripp Umbach, 2010, p. 2).

Further, state and local leaders look to universities to step up partnerships for strengthening community well-being, in a sense asking the university to "defin[e] its role in community engagement as undertaking strategic community revitalization with specific neighborhood(s) through reciprocal, enduring, and diverse partnerships" (Vidal et al., 2002, p. vii; Shaffer & Wright, 2010). By alleviating poverty in the surrounding community or increasing the educational achievement of area children, community and university leaders build stronger, more welcoming communities. University participation is not, however, completely altruistic. In many instances, institutional leaders act from an enlightened self-interest. Undoubtedly, reducing poverty and increasing educational attainment does improve the community, but one can question whether or not the university entered into the partnership to contribute to the community's new vision for itself or to enhance its own ability to recruit and retain students, faculty, and administrative professionals (Maurrasse, 2001).

Sorting out this complex mix of motivations may in the end be impossible. Evaluating the impact of engagement on a particular community requires examining the process through which the partnership goals were established. Community development scholars question the effects of community revitalization through economic development because of the potential to disenfranchise local residents (Barker & Brown, 2009; Bridger & Alter, 2006). Enacting engagement as a process requires universities and their individual representatives to cultivate a sense of themselves as members of a community and to participate in building this shared vision. In doing so, university actors support the revitalization of communities and also enjoy the benefits of safe, desirable neighborhoods.

Reconciling Competing Roles: The Anchor Institution Mission

Community–university partnerships addressing community health and university participation in economic development activities are often seen—and therefore have been presented in this chapter—as separate activities for higher education institutions; they are also sometimes discussed as competing goals. Recent writing positions the university as an economic actor, as above. Indeed, in the United States' 100 largest cities, the business activities of a university and/or a hospital represent one of the largest forces shaping local and regional economics (Hecht, 2012). In October, 2011, Secretary of Housing and Urban Development Shaun Donovan spoke to a group of urban leaders and business executives at the CEOs for Cities conference in Chicago. He focused his remarks on HUD's ideas for growing cities and regions; in essence, he pointed to "eds and meds" and other institutions *anchored* in a particular city/region that might translate into drivers of economic growth for that place (Bergen, 2011). This idea of linking the future well-being of a particular place to successful collaborations with particular types of entities has taken the community–university partnerships common for more than a century to a new place, and situated the university as a key component in first stabilizing and then revitalizing communities (Hodges & Dubb, 2012; Maurrasse, 2001).

Hodges and Dubb (2012) use the term *anchor institution movement* to denote the growing trend among colleges and universities to recognize and act upon their responsibilities as anchors in the local or regional economy. In pursuing an anchor institution mission "the full range of university activities

---

are important" (Hodges & Dubb, 2012, p. xiv). Partnerships with public schools support educational attainment. Universities invest in communities by buying from local merchants and hiring neighborhood residents. Real estate development plans, for example, provide opportunities for universities to invest real dollars in the community, so as to better meet the educational and research functions of the institution.

In the interest of "mov[ing] beyond promotion, public relations and anecdotes," Hodges and Dubb (2012) offer a typology based on the case studies of the roles 10 universities play in cities such as Cincinnati, Memphis, New Haven, Portland, and Indianapolis (p. xxv). Universities acting as *facilitators* support many partnerships, across a variety of sectors, and several different neighborhoods. Miami Dade College, Portland State University, and University of Indiana-Purdue University at Indianapolis, all acting from an institutional commitment to community well-being, support service-learning projects, volunteerism, and community–university partnerships across their metropolitan areas to address, primarily, education and public health issues. Other institutions act as *leaders*, applying significant institutional resources to the revitalization of low-income neighborhoods with an eye to improving safety and quality of life for the university's students and employees. The University of Cincinnati, Yale University, and the University of Pennsylvania share a common attribute: high crime rates in neighborhoods adjacent to the campus. Each of these institutions has taken an active leadership role in the surrounding area to address these issues. While community stakeholders are typically consulted by leader institutions in developing appropriate strategies, university administrators retain most of the decision-making authority as they allocate institutional funds and dedicate staff to particular initiatives. Other campus leaders act as *conveners* in nonadjacent neighborhoods, convening cross-sector partnerships aimed at addressing community-based concerns (pp. xiv–xv, 11–16). LeMoyne-Owen College, the University of Minnesota, Syracuse University, and Emory University work in concert with municipal, civic, business, and social service entities to revitalize particular neighborhoods/areas within their city. The categories in Hodges and Dubb's typology are not mutually exclusive; it is, however, typical for an individual institution to take primarily one approach over others, as dictated by that institution's mission and administrative priorities.

Unbalanced focus on economic development of communities risks "increased inequality and divisiveness" (Bridger & Alter, 2006, p. 171). Rutheiser (2012), manager for the Annie E. Casey Foundation's anchor institution initiatives, acknowledges the same with regard to the anchor institution movement:

> [W]ithout a clear "anchor institution mission" that strategically deploys the economic, human, and intellectual capital of institutions to improve the long-term welfare of the communities in which they reside, the growth of universities by themselves will not necessarily improve circumstances for the people who live in distressed communities adjacent to these institutions and, indeed, could make conditions worse. (p. x)

Rutheiser cautions institutional leaders against an overemphasis on "the growth of universities by themselves," referring to strategies that might advance the institution's self-interest without considering the needs or desires of the surrounding community. For example, local critics of the University of Pennsylvania's efforts to rebuild West Philadelphia and the University City neighborhood call those efforts "Penntrification," and have in the past worried that national chain stores moving into the neighborhood will threaten the livelihood of locally owned businesses (Drummond, 2009).

Implicit in the scholarship related to community–university interactions is the critical nature of the relationships built among participants; the success of the partnership depends upon them. Strong relationships between Penn and its neighbors in University City could support the community in addressing their concerns. Schneekloth and Shibley (1995) discuss placemaking as synonymous with relationship building. "Social change, environmental change and management, and competent research in the practice of placemaking occur," they say, "when there is a congruence between the various goals of people affected by this place" (p. 9). That congruence of goals is not a matter of happenstance; rather, as Schneekloth and Shibley remind campus leaders, "it must be nurtured" (p. 9). Nurturing these relationships is "a complex task . . . rooted in fully appreciating the context of each professional interaction" (p. 9). Such an endeavor requires a commitment to deliberative practices as the basis for relationships with community members. In higher education institutions, these will require organizational and cultural changes.

To achieve the shift from engagement as product to engagement as process advocated in this monograph, university actors will need to explore a series of issues currently challenging their ability to embrace the reunderstood engagement ethos discussed in the first chapter. This monograph is presented in the format of a research proposal, suggesting that further study might advance institutional and individual efforts to make the move from outcome to process. The second, third, and fourth chapters operate, in effect, as reviews of particular body of literature related to community–university engagement. As in a research proposal, we come to the end of such a literature review with a clearer sense of the gaps in the literature, and foci for future research projects. When community is framed as neighborhood, a place where residents collaborate to change the community, we see aspects of university structure and functioning that inhibit engagement as a process. The examples of community–university interaction presented in this chapter invite institutional change related to mission and particularly operating structures in order to effect a new approach to engaging with a broad representation of the community.

Directions for Future Research: Institutional Change

When campus leaders intentionally move to enact an anchor institution mission, or indeed "any, or all forms of engagement," they typically do so in a move away from standard operating procedures (Hodges & Dubb, 2012, p. 27). Accordingly, leaders would be well served to draw on the results of empirical research related to institutional change at colleges and universities successfully prioritizing engagement as the process by which institutional actors engage with members of the surrounding community. Further, the literature related to adaptive leadership will provide important insights about possible approaches to manage change (Heifetz & Laurie, 1997; Randall & Coakley, 2007). Senior leaders might begin by reviewing the existing literature. For example, the institutions Hodges and Dubb highlighted "have begun to see themselves as part of their surrounding community," and come to understand "their futures [as] intertwined with the success of their neighbors" (p. 27). Creating an engaged community will, their findings suggest, require changing the way the university understands its relationship to its physical surroundings and, perhaps more fundamentally, the institutional culture itself (Kezar, 2011; Ramaley & Holland, 2005). One implication of this line of scholarship is clear: institutional change is necessary to facilitate building and maintaining strong relationships with partners, or engagement as a process (McNall et al., 2009). Without such change, engagement will remain an outcome, or product, accomplished as possible within existing structures.

Effecting change on this order requires skilled leadership. Organizational learning and adaptive leadership approaches may support campus-level culture change, and therefore warrant attention here. University actors will also benefit from examples of other institutional leaders who have successfully implemented change, such as Judith Ramaley's story of change leadership at Portland State University presented here. The chapter concludes with a discussion of research methodologies that might be employed to inform institutional change initiatives.

Leadership

Faculty at so-called engaged universities often portray their provost or president as an engagement champion who transformed a campus by creating or advancing a strong culture of engagement (Moore & Ward, 2010). Transformational leaders such as these rely on their personal charisma to achieve broad commitment to change, motivating individuals to achieve what might otherwise have seemed impossible in a given organizational context (Randall & Coakley, 2007). Transactional leaders use rewards to motivate specific acts of change; however, such an approach may be difficult to sustain in institutions where resources are limited (Pounder, 2001). Transformational leaders are not hampered by resource constraints; rather, their efforts are hindered by

Adaptive Challenge:

their tremendous responsibility to sustain change that may not withstand a particular person's departure from the institution (Randall & Coakley, 2007).

Embracing a role as placemaker and acting from an anchor institution mission represent transformative change initiatives for colleges and universities because these activities do not align with the traditional culture, attitudes, and functioning of higher education institutions. Accordingly, colleges and universities spurred into community–university engagement face adaptive challenges, systemic difficulties in current operating approaches brought on by change in the surrounding environment, much like the changes experienced by higher education institutions now being asked to engage more directly with community members (Heifetz & Laurie, 1997). Making the shift from viewing engagement as an outcome of faculty or administrative effort to embracing a relational approach to interactions between community and university representatives presents an adaptive challenge to an individual institution, and invites constituents across the partnerships to embrace a process of change.

Change as a Scholarly Act

Even with empirical data in hand, changing the structure of an individual higher education institution could be a daunting task. Many have suggested that such an endeavor is somewhat futile, particularly given that "higher education institutions do not seem to learn from their mistakes," as evidenced, for example, by a university that has previously implemented a new technology and experienced negative results, then adopts a second untried innovation (Kezar, 2005a, p. 1). Criticisms such as this assume that the university as an organization, distinct from the individual actors within the institution, can learn and that new knowledge/learning becomes embedded in the organizational systems themselves, transcending the individual people who move through positions as their career changes (Kezar, 2005b; Senge, 1990). Positioning the university as a learning organization may provide valuable tools for changing administrative practice, as well as fostering partnerships (Anderson, 2005). Such a shift in thinking about how the university does or can function would, from Anderson's perspective, precede focused efforts on a particular outcome such as increased engagement with the surrounding community.

Portland State University provides an example of a learning organization changing its administrative practice to support a new approach to engagement. Responding to a perceived budget crisis in the early 1990s, new president Judith Ramaley led the campus through a period of change that required significant organizational learning (Ramaley, 2002; Ramaley & Holland, 2005). PSU leaders framed transformational change as a scholarly act (Ramaley, 2000), and began with a thorough review of the empirical literature as well as institutional research data specifically related to the issue at hand. By doing so, campus leaders created a compelling case for action that changed administrative practice as well as campus culture (Ramaley, 2002), and ultimately transformed Portland State University into a national leader in the anchor institution movement. This story reflects many important ideas relevant to the discussion in this chapter, as well as suggesting directions for future research. First, wide-ranging change may be/likely is necessary to realize institutional goals for engagement as a process for interacting rather than simply an outcome of institutional efforts. Further, individual actors might resist change. However, inherent characteristics of universities and their constituents can be turned into assets in the change management process; namely, at Portland State, leaders framed change as a scholarly act and thereby drew faculty and academic administrators into research focused on organizational change. Ramaley and Holland (2005) justify this approach as "consistent with academic culture" (p. 77); scholars more readily participated in the change process that had been carefully grounded in the processes of social science research, including at PSU a thorough review of the literature on engagement and on organizational change.

Methodologies to Advance Institutional Change

Despite individual examples like the Portland State story, many administrators and scholars dismiss the learning organization framework as a management fad, and eschew organizational learning strategies (Kezar, 2005b; Senge, 1990). Doing so may set aside promising tools for reshaping the culture and practice of higher education. Action research (AR) traditions offer many possible research methodologies for investigating how organizations learn to operate in new ways and evaluating the efficacy of framing an institution as a learning organization. AR is a cyclical process beginning with identifying a current concern in a particular environment. In this case, the issue is the need for organizational change to facilitate an engagement-as-process approach to community–university interactions. University leaders engaged in action research could make some change to the operating procedures, and then use action research methods to monitor the action/change by gathering data about what's happening. Evaluation of the new approach provides empirical evidence to be used to modify the practice in light of the evaluation (Kemmis & McTaggart, 2005). Glassman, Erdem, and Bartholomew (2012) describe AR as a social change tool, focusing on patterns of interaction within a community. I take university to be synonymous with learning organization, and I think of a learning organization as a community of individual learners. A necessary first step in changing organizational practices is to identify the accepted practices and structural barriers that inhibit universities from being responsive to community-driven change (Glassman et al., 2012). For example, funding for a new public health intervention might be awarded to a university researcher through a federal grant or contract. Students in a particular course could staff a literacy program as part of a service-learning project. Standard operating procedures at the university might make it difficult for the community organization to receive funds from the grant or cover its services outside the 16-week semester (Ward, 2003). If so, changes can be made to the process to advance a shift to engagement as process. In turn, AR offers a promising approach for evaluating the new process, making adjustments and moving forward.

The need to effect organizational change within individual colleges and universities stems from two ideas at the heart of this monograph. One, overemphasis on economic development in communities threatens to undermine development of community capacity to lead development efforts and to disenfranchise further members of underrepresented groups such as those of lower socioeconomic status, racial minorities, youth, and the elderly (Bridger & Alter, 2006). Two, universities, and their individual representatives, are members of the community where the institution is located and as such they are important participants in community development. To realize their role as supporters of community-driven change, university actors must move away from engaging for the sake of being able to adopt the *engaged campus* moniker, and adopt engagement as a process for interacting with other members of the community.

Community as Classroom

COLLEGE AND UNIVERSITY students contribute to the geographically defined communities where they live during their college career through course-based and cocurricular activities; they will also play important roles in the communities where they live and work after graduation. Because the contributions made by individual citizens are important to communities, university faculty and administrators have emphasized preparing students as civic leaders as another response to the call for increased engagement described in the previous chapters. Scholars and practitioners have, in turn, written widely about approaches to and outcomes of service-learning as the primary pedagogy of the community–university engagement movement (Cress, Burack, Giles, Elkins, & Stevens, 2010). Faculty, in their role as teachers, have adopted service-learning approaches to connect experiential learning activities with course content through structured reflection activities (Eyler & Giles, 1999). Students in a course on juvenile delinquency at the University of Indiana-Purdue University at Indianapolis (IUPUI) completed a service-learning project providing mentoring for incarcerated youth transitioning back to their home community upon release from a detention facility; through these experiences, the IUPUI students learned firsthand from transitioning youth about patterns of delinquency as well as the challenges of reintegrating into their home community and avoiding triggers to reoffend. First-year engineering students at Louisiana State University explored principles of engineering through a partnership with the Baton Rouge School District focused on designing playgrounds for elementary schools. Both instructors received national recognition from service-learning organizations and their academic disciplinary associations for these projects, which have been promoted as best practice models. Through service-learning experiences such as these, students can connect what they learn in the college classroom with the people, experiences, and places beyond the campus where the concepts will ultimately be applied.

Service-learning is not the only method through which students and university educators interact with their communities. Beyond their academic coursework, students can participate in a wide variety of community-based experiential learning opportunities during their university career, including cocurricular leadership development and citizen education activities (Kendall, 1990; Stanton, Giles, & Cruz, 1999). Student services professionals offer community service activities such as the Big Event, a nationwide day of service drawing students into university communities to build houses with Habitat for Humanity, clean up neighborhoods, and collect food for food pantries. Leadership development programs, blending community service with academic coursework focused on principles of leadership, invite students to reflect on providing leadership for community-building initiatives (Keen & Hall, 2009). National initiatives, such as the American Democracy Project sponsored by the American Association of State Colleges and Universities, invite students and faculty to adopt service-learning and also to engage in discussions of current events as reported in the *New York Times*.

When educators and their students connect with people, experiences, and places beyond the campus in these various ways, teachers and learners frame community as a classroom where formal and informal learning takes place. Doing so has implications for all involved in these encounters because the classroom metaphor holds such considerable power in the public imagination (Plater, 1995). The word *classroom* traditionally evokes specific images: a space inside a building, on a campus, set aside for learning structured by a recognized expert (i.e., a university faculty member) and free of distraction. The community–university engagement movement "tak[es] the [classroom] door off its hinges," challenging images of the college classroom as a sacred place separate from the real world (Zlotkowski, 2001, p. 26). By framing community as a learning space, the engagement movement also acknowledges the expertise of community members as teachers (Plater, 1995).

This chapter begins by considering the prevailing rhetoric about the intended outcomes of (a) higher education. Where one stands on that issue has dictated subsequent attitudes regarding if, how, and to what end students should engage with their community, and therefore the question of intended outcomes is treated here separately from discussion of the role of higher education institutions. By distinguishing the role and the purpose of higher education, I am also intentionally highlighting twin responsibilities for colleges and universities. Universities must prepare employees and also educate citizens. To that end, this chapter focuses on teaching for active citizenship, community experiences with civic engagement, and finally the issues of institutional purpose brought to the fore when community is understood as a classroom.

Intended Outcomes of (a) Higher Education

Concerns about the U.S. economy and its global competitiveness emerged in the 1980s; at that time, leaders in government and industry looked to higher education institutions to produce graduates who were more and better prepared for working in a new economic climate (Newman, 1985). Two distinct ideas about the purpose, or intended outcomes, of a college education are evident in this discourse. One emphasizes citizenship education, and the other focuses on preparing for the global workforce, framing higher education alternatively as a public or a private good.

The public good argument is straightforward: College "educate[s] citizens"; along the way to earning a degree, individuals must also prepare to assume "their political roles both as members and agents of the body politic" (Cadwallader, 1982, p. 404). From a public good perspective, educating future civic leaders is particularly important given the documented decline of student interest and participation in politics in the decades prior to the 2008 presidential election (The National Task Force on Civic Learning and Democratic Engagement, 2012). This decline has been a source of ongoing concern; a decade earlier, the American Political Science Association Task Force (1998) painted this decline as "threatening the vitality and stability of democratic politics in the United States" and called for more civic education (p. 636; see also Colby, Beaumont, Ehrlich, & Corngold, 2007; Skocpol

& Fiorina, 1999). Empirical evidence suggests a link between college curriculum and civic participation (Galston, 2001). Although the results are mixed, some scholars have presented evidence that community-oriented habits, such as political participation, civic engagement, and social activism developed in college, persist after graduation (Adler & Goggin, 2005; Colby et al., 2007; Pascarella, Salisbury, Martin, & Blaich, 2012).

The private good frame emphasizes the preparation of college graduates as members of the global workforce in the knowledge-based economy (The National Leadership Council for Liberal Education and America's Promise, 2007). The primary role of higher education institutions, from this perspective, is as a work force development resource. Consistent with this, then U.S. Secretary of Education, Margaret Spellings convened a 19-member commission in 2006 "[t]o consider how best to improve our system of higher education, to ensure that our graduates are well prepared to meet our future workforce needs and are able to participate fully in the changing economy" (Spellings Commission, 2006, p. 33). Higher education institutions, from this perspective, enhance the public good by promoting the private good through educating individuals who will in turn use their education to increase their earning power, thereby contributing more in tax revenue and personal resources (time in volunteer/community building activities, etc.) to the community.

Participants in a recent national gathering recognized the undergraduate years as a time replete with unique opportunities to help students see more expansive relationships between the public and private missions of higher education. Emphasizing the importance of education for democratic citizenship, members of the National Task Force on Civic Learning and Democratic Engagement (2012) called democracy "much more than a design for . . . lawmaking. Rather, it is a framework for a special kind of society in which citizens must take mutual responsibility for the quality of their own communities and their shared lives" (p. 22). Sustaining or improving communities calls for ensuring that basic human needs are being met for all, and also that there are public spaces and deliberative processes in place that welcome everyone in the community to participate. The economic well-being of the community matters in ensuring these things, and therefore the employability of students/future workers matters, too. Accordingly, the American Association of Colleges and Universities, along with many other scholars and organizations, has called for a revamping of the college curriculum to create civic learning opportunities more relevant to the changing world and to prepare students for the work of public life and community building (Musil, 2011; The National Task Force on Civic Learning and Democratic Engagement, 2012).

When engagement is the desired process for community–university interaction, advancing the public and the private good are not competing aims for the university. Neither are educating citizens and preparing workers mutually exclusive. Each of the two positions overlooks important elements of the other worldview. Single-minded focus on public good ignores economic realities and may not adequately provide all citizens with opportunities to earn a living wage or provide other basic needs for themselves and/or their families. On the other hand, a growing U.S. economy in the first decade of the 21st century has led directly to increased income disparity, further disenfranchising those in the lowest socioeconomic stratum (Wolff, 2011). The National Task Force on Civic Learning called on future graduates to share responsibility for the physical place where they live and for the social relationships among all those who live there. To respond to this call, graduates require solid academic preparation in a chosen field as well as the skills and disposition for active citizenship.

Teaching and Learning for Civic Engagement

When we think about how to educate for global citizenship or to prepare future employees for the knowledge economy, service-learning projects come readily to mind as one way to achieve these goals. The label *service-learning*, in the 1980s and 1990s, often referred generally to a variety of community-based experiential learning activities ranging from community service and volunteerism to internships and fieldwork. By the mid 1990s, the scholarship reflected a new consensus: all activities linking students and community members did not equally promote the same kinds of student learning outcomes (Eyler & Giles, 1999; Furco, 1996); service-learning came to refer much more specifically to academic course-based learning featuring opportunities for structured reflection on the connections between the service and the course content. However, in the last 10 years, scholars are pointing out the limitations of *service-learning* as an eponymous label for community-engaged learning, given the wide variety of curricular and cocurricular activities beyond those described earlier in this chapter which can foster student development as active citizens (Smith, Nowacek, & Bernstein, 2010). Saltmarsh and Zlotkowski (2011) suggest instead *civic engagement* to encompass various curricular and cocurricular teaching and learning modalities positioning community as a classroom; throughout this monograph, I have respected individual authors' choice of language and use *civic engagement* to describe any of the wide variety of ways in which students can and do prepare for their roles as active citizens. The following section examines the various categories of student civic engagement activities individually, first to overview the empirical basis for arguments about the impact of college on future citizens and, second, to make two final points about student learning outcomes of civic engagement in general, and the experiences of participating communities and the individual community members involved.

Cocurricular Civic Engagement

The Campus Outreach Opportunity League (COOL), founded in the mid-1980s by Harvard University alumnus Wayne Meisel, is one of the oldest campus organizations dedicated to facilitating community service and civic engagement opportunities for students (Liu, 1996; Meisel & Hackett, 1986). COOL helped Harvard students address social and community issues in the greater Boston metropolitan area through volunteering and community service activities; in this sense, COOL was a typical student organization focused on volunteer activities for individuals and groups. These community service opportunities are synonymous with *service-learning* (Rhoads, 1998, pp. 279–280). Where service-learning is explicitly positioned as the pedagogy of the civic engagement movement, students are exploring academic concepts in the context of community as a formal classroom. Cocurricular and other experiential learning opportunities such as student leadership programs featuring community service activities also present learning opportunities in the community as an informal classroom (Bonsall, Harris, & Marczak, 2002; Dugan, 2006).

Today, many community service activities have been subsumed under the aegis of student leadership programs (Komives, Lucas, & McMahon, 2006). Fifteen years ago, as scholars and practitioners sorted out the distinctions among various civic engagement activities and their possible outcomes, Perreault (1997) advanced what she called the "citizen leader" framework for student engagement to foster active citizenship. Through this approach, students learn to see themselves as "concerned citizens" who, along with other residents, seek to effect positive change in their communities (p. 151). Her approach connects with other calls for expanded citizen involvement in public work and the promise of the university to draw students into their roles as active citizens (Barker & Brown, 2009; Boyte, 2008). Subsequent research on the impact of various kinds of civic engagement activities, including these cocurricular opportunities, has repeatedly emphasized the importance of structured reflection and intentional connection to broader curricular learning objectives (Keen & Hall, 2008, 2009). Experiences more overtly connected with the academic curriculum provide more support for achieving student outcomes in a variety of areas (Warren, 2012).

(Academically Based) Service-Learning

While the civic engagement movement is widely considered to have its roots in social justice activism of the 1960s and 1970s (Liu, 1996; Stanton et al., 1999), the term *service-learning* originates in community economic development projects during Lyndon Johnson's War on Poverty. Robert Sigmon and his colleagues at the Southern Regional Education Board (1973) first used the term to describe the work of student volunteers in the Tennessee Valley between 1968 and 1973. Several authors carefully differentiated service-learning from other activities by insisting on mutual learning and mutual benefit for both student and community organizations as characteristics of community service learning experiences (Bringle & Hatcher, 1996; Furco, 1996).

By the late 1990s, the tone of the civic engagement literature reflected a broad consensus about the value of service-learning as a pedagogical tool (Saltmarsh & Zlotkowski, 2011). The consensus faltered around the intended outcomes of the educational experience. This argument mirrored the dialectical nature of the ideological roots of service-learning and civic engagement, reflecting philosophical differences, or what Zlotkowski (1995) referred to as the "ideological biases" of the movement's pioneers (p. 123; see also Stanton et al., 1999). One group argued for harnessing the university's resources "to serve a larger [democratic] purpose" (Boyer, 1996, p. 20; see also Saltmarsh & Hartley, 2011). Others saw service-learning less as a tool for social change than as a powerful pedagogy to advance discipline-based academic learning.

DiPadova-Stocks (2005) points to four principle issues cycling through the literature on academically based service-learning across two decades: defining service-learning; doing it effectively; measuring the outcomes; and assessing the impacts, on students and on communities. A thorough review of the literature in each or even any one of these areas is outside the scope of this monograph. Conway, Amel, and Gerwein's (2009) meta-analysis of more than 75 studies explores the effect of service-learning on academic, personal, social, and citizenship outcomes for K–20 students and other adult learners. Their results confirm the crucial link between course design and student learning outcomes. Teaching for active citizenship also requires attention to related impacts of civic engagement on communities. This section offers suggestions for further reading for those interested in exploring any of these topics more thoroughly.

Course Design. The earliest literature on service-learning included reports from instructors on how they integrated the pedagogy into their courses and the outcomes of these decisions. Explicitly connecting service-learning to formal courses in which the student had a particular interest (i.e., in their major field of study) seemed—in the early literature—to have greater impact on desired student outcomes than did other forms of community service (Astin, Vogelgesang, Ikeda, & Yee, 2000; Vogelgesang & Astin, 2000). Further, longer periods of service, such as those embedded in a particular course, led to more positive outcomes than short-term volunteering or community service experiences (Berger & Milem, 2002; Knapp, Fisher, & Levesque-Bristol, 2010). Scholars continue to offer support for these initial findings (Battistoni, Longo, & Jayanandhan, 2009; Einfield & Collins, 2008; Engberg & Fox, 2011). Based on three decades of research, two elements make the most difference in terms of student outcomes. Rigorous reflection has been repeatedly demonstrated to be the most important element of service-learning course design, from the perspective of achieving desired outcomes (Conway et al., 2009; Felten & Clayton, 2011).

Students especially need formal opportunities for reflection as part of the civic engagement experience when they encounter unfamiliar or uncomfortable situations (Diaz & Perrault, 2010; Keen & Hall, 2008, 2009; Knapp et al., 2010). This is a well-established tenet of the field; Eyler and Giles (1999) consider reflection critical for the resolution of cognitive dissonance students may experience when serving in a setting different from their previous experiences. Motivation to bring about structural change is another possible positive outcome of structured reflection activities. Ash and Clayton (2004) offer the "articulated learning" model; through this approach, students describe the civic engagement experience, analyze this experience in the context of the course material/relevant phenomenon, and articulate the learning they have experienced (p. 135; for evaluation rubric, see Ash, Clayton, & Atkinson, 2005). This model for reflection "clearly demonstrates rather than reports learning; pushes students beyond superficial interpretations of complex issues; and facilitates academic mastery, personal growth, civic engagement and critical thinking" (Ash & Clayton, 2004, p. 140). Teaching students to develop comfort with repeated structured reflection is "central to creating a habit of questioning and integrating experience and subject matter" (Eyler & Giles, 1999, p. 146).

Another element of course design frequently mentioned in the literature is the instructor's approach to issues of diversity, and students' racial and/or socioeconomic privilege. Indeed, service-learning may not be an appropriate teaching strategy, if it is not possible to mitigate negative impacts of Whiteness or other forms of privilege on service-learners' attitudes (Catlett & Proweller, 2011; Endres & Gould, 2009; Stoecker & Tryon, 2009). Engaging with difference does "matter," as it supports key personal and professional learning outcomes (Keen & Hall, 2009, p. 59; Buch & Harden, 2011; Holsapple, 2012). Accordingly, careful thought must be given to designing civic engagement experiences so as to support students in exploring differences while also coming to understand their own experiences of privilege (Seider & Hillman, 2011).

Civic Education. "Civic mindedness," a quality institutions seek to nurture through civic education efforts, is "a person's inclination or disposition to be knowledgeable of and involved in the community, and to have a commitment to act up a sense of responsibility as a member of that community" (Bringle & Steinberg, 2010, p. 429). The "civic-minded graduate" is one who "has the capacity and desire to work with others to achieve the common good" (p. 429). The 10 domains of the civic-minded graduate reflect the comprehensive list of learning outcomes identified in previously published studies on civic engagement in higher education (Bringle & Steinberg, 2010, pp. 430–436; Steinberg, Hatcher, & Bringle, 2011, p. 22). Cocurricular civic engagement and academically based service-learning both have been demonstrated repeatedly to foster civic learning and may, if designed intentionally, support the development of civic-minded graduates (Steinberg et al., 2011).

Student Learning Outcomes
The scholarship related to civic engagement discusses a variety of learning outcomes, ranging from discipline-specific knowledge to the cognitive and psychosocial development which occurs during the college years for traditionally aged college students. Students have the opportunity to experience public places, social spaces, and specific issues as connected with their learning in such a way as to make a two-fold difference in their education: Discipline-specific, academic learning outcomes are facilitated in a profound way through educative experiences (Dewey, 1933), and students practice citizenship skills upon which communities depend (Scobey, 2010).

Early scholarship documented the positive impact of "community service" on student academic learning and personal development (e.g., Markus, Howard, & King, 1993). Positive correlations between service and academic learning continued to be strong across several longitudinal studies conducted by researchers at UCLA's Higher Education Research Institution, using data from the CIRP Freshman Survey (Astin & Sax, 1998; Astin, Sax, & Avalos, 1999; Astin et al., 2000; Vogelgesang & Astin, 2000). Service-learning in particular "is seen to enhance students outcomes (cognitive, affective and ethical), foster a more active citizenry, . . ., support a more equitable society and reconnect K–16 schools with their local communities" (Butin, 2003, p. 1675).

Learning Outcomes. Beginning with Cohen and Kinsey's (1994) survey of 217 communication students, Warren (2012) considered the 11 extant studies that have examined the impact of service-learning on some aspect of student learning. She notes a variety of positive effects, "including cultural awareness, social responsibility, and student cognitive learning outcomes" (p. 59). Continued research and theory development are warranted, to further explicate the precise elements of the service-learning experience that effects learning not achieved in a traditional course design.

Engberg and Fox (2011) offered a meta-analysis of the literature linking a broader array of civic engagement activities and various cognitive and psychosocial measures. In doing so, they demonstrate that service-learning contributes to two aspects of cognitive development: linguistic, cultural, and academic knowledge; and analysis of multiple perspectives, critical thinking, and problem solving (e.g., Battistoni et al., 2009; Einfeld & Collins, 2008; Jay, 2008; Jones & Abes, 2004; Lechuga, Clerc, & Howell, 2009; Morgan & Streb, 2001; Rockquemore & Schaffer, 2000). Students develop intrapersonal dimensions as well. Identity, self-awareness, confidence, and sense of empowerment are increased through civic activities, as are tolerance of and interest in diversity and ambiguity (Lechuga et al., 2009; Moely, McFarland, Miron, Mercer, & Ilustre, 2002). Civic engagement also fosters student interpersonal development on two fronts: acquiring skills such as empathy and trust; and strengthening educational, career, and social commitments (e.g., Battistoni et al., 2009; Engberg & Mayhew, 2007; Jay, 2008; Jones & Abes, 2004; Keen & Hall, 2009; Mayhew & Engberg, 2011; Moely, Furco, & Reed, 2008).

Not all reviewers are positive. Eby (1998) judged the service-learning movement as "bad" because, in part, service-learning can, and sometimes does, reinforce negative stereotypes held by service-learners about members of the community in which they are serving. While this is certainly an element of course design requiring careful attention per the previous discussion, the preponderance of empirical evidence on the topic suggests that the stereotypes students held diminished as a result of interaction with diverse others (see Holsapple's [2012] meta-analysis of the literature related to the diversity outcomes of civic engagement for further discussion of this body of literature). Students' tolerance of difference increases through service-learning and civic engagement opportunities; their level of comfort in cross-cultural interactions also increased. Intergroup dialogue and other opportunities to reflect individually and with diverse others support intra- and interpersonal growth in this area (Diaz & Perrault, 2010). Although Holsapple's analysis generally supports the premise that service learners experience positive diversity outcomes, he expresses several concerns with the various elements of the methodology in the studies reviewed, which in turn limit the trustworthiness of the findings. Continued research, with attention to sampling procedures and data sources, is necessary so as to provide empirical foundation for best practices in teaching for diversity outcomes.

Impact of Personal Characteristics. Course design impacts significantly the outcome of civic engagement on student learning and on cognitive and psychosocial development. Targeting specific outcomes, providing ample opportunities for structured reflection through dialogue or writing, and the length of service are all critical elements of course design. Evidence suggests that personal characteristics of the service-learner also impacts outcomes. Eyler and Giles's (1999) analysis suggested that the gender of the service learner impacted outcomes; they report finding that women experienced more, more positive changes as a result of civic engagement than did male students. The changes included knowing themselves better (p. 280), feeling intellectually challenged by and learning more from the experience (p. 281), and reframing issues as a result of the service experience (p. 282). Eyler and Giles found little evidence of the effect of other individual characteristics such as minority status, age, and family income. More recent works contradict this, suggesting racial/ethnic identity, as well as gender, influences the impact of civic engagement on learning and developmental outcomes, given that "women and students of color experience service-learning differently than their male and White counterparts" (Engberg & Fox, 2011, p. 90; see also Einfeld & Collins, 2008; Green, 2001; Jones & Abes, 2004; Novick, Seider, & Huguley, 2011; Seider, Huguley, & Novick, 2013). While Novick et al. (2011) did not see the outcomes of civic engagement differ by race/ethnicity per se, the interpretations that students/participants in their study offered of their experiences did.

Individual differences in meaning making is evident in Lee's (2005) study of the experiences of participants ($n = 94$) in an academically based service-learning project. Although she set out to examine socioeconomic class as a mediator in service-learning experiences, students' class and racial identity became conflated in the findings in the sense that, particularly among students from lower socioeconomic class backgrounds, participants specifically mentioned the racial composition of the communities where they served when discussing their experiences. Frequently, the service learners drew connections between their own racial/ethnic identity and that of the community's residents. This did not, it warrants acknowledging, hold true for all students of color; one Latino from a middle-/upper-class family background spoke to this: "I knew that my advice only ran so deep because of the difference between our lives" (p. 319). Lee's findings speak to the design of service-learning opportunities: sharing socioeconomic class backgrounds with individuals or communities served may be more salient than shared racial or ethnic identity. These findings are also very important in the context of the impact of service-learning on communities, a topic of "noted, and suspicious, absence" (Bortolin, 2011, p. 49) in the scholarship of civic engagement.

One possible explanation for limited focus on community impact in the scholarship is the debate in the 1990s about the role of civic engagement for students and institutions (Saltmarsh & Zlotkowski, 2011). Some linked service-learning with social change motivations; this perspective would presumably support paying sustained attention to the effect of particular activities on the communities where they took place. Others valued civic engagement for its efficacy in promoting academic discipline- or program-specific learning objectives, and focused on the student as the unit of analysis when evaluating civic engagement initiatives. On the whole, the scholarship reviewed above reflects the second perspective. Given the university's role as an educator, the effects of civic engagement on students cannot be ignored. As universities make the shift from product- to process-oriented engagement, faculty and academic administrators alike will benefit from recognizing the many "teachable moments" that occur at the confluence of course content and lived experience and take this opportunity to clarify abstract concepts and to demonstrate their relevance to students' lives (Ravitch, 2007, p. 211). These are opportunities to draw students' attention to how they interact with community partners and other residents, and to others' experiences of civic engagement activities.

Community Experiences of Civic Engagement

Surveying the early scholarship on service-learning and civic engagement, Cruz and Giles (2000) asked a critical question: Where's the community in community service-learning? This question is still pertinent, more than a decade later (Giles, 2010). Certainly, since their challenge, more attention has been given to understanding the experience of community agency personnel who host service-learning students (Bushouse, 2005; Sandy & Holland, 2006). The findings from these few studies are mixed.

Worrall (2007) uncovered many benefits, as well as challenges, experienced by community agencies hosting service-learners from DePaul University's Stearns Center for Community-Based Service-Learning. Benefits included: DePaul students served as positive role models for youth in the programs; parents learned about DePaul and had the opportunity to think of it as a college option for their child. Students also brought enthusiasm, new perspectives/ideas, and a basic skill set one might expect from a college student, thereby requiring less training. Having service-learners covering some of the agencies' activities extended those agencies' budgets, allowing them to hire additional program staff; the volunteer hours dedicated by the service-learners could also be leveraged as in-kind donations for the purposes of grant proposals and other funding requests. Hosting service-learning students was not, however, without its challenges. The DePaul University academic term is 10 weeks long; agencies struggled to develop a system for rotating students into and out of volunteer placements so as to minimize the disruption of services to their clients. Several directors also expressed a desire to have closer contact with faculty members and the opportunity to think together about other ways that both the agency and the students might benefit from the relationship. The challenges experienced by DePaul's partner agencies resembled those of peers who hosted students from other institutions: for example, Blouin and Perry (2009) list the key challenges for agencies, which included "issues related to student conduct, poor fit between course and organizational objectives, and lack of communication between instructors and organizations" (p. 120). Nonetheless, agencies partnering with DePaul University and participating in this case study clearly felt that the benefits gained by their organizations more than offset the challenges.

Community agency directors in both Worrall's (2007) study and in Sandy and Holland's (2006) focus groups saw themselves as part of the teaching team. "[A] great partnership," one director told Sandy and Holland, "is when you stop saying MY students. They're OUR students. What are OUR needs? We share these things in common, so let's go for it" (emphasis in original, p. 30). Some participants embraced an educator role because they considered it critical to the future of their home communities. The executive director of a community-based agency in Chicago thought of himself as teaching future policy makers; as such, he focused on giving service learners "a better understanding of what it is to be a Latino or a poor person in these communities, so . . . they can have a true understanding of what impact their [future] decisions will have" on individuals and/or communities (Worrall, 2007, p. 10). It is important, though, to note that the findings outlined here may well be unique to these institutions and communities, reinforcing the salience of place in the study of civic engagement as outlined in the previous chapter.

Based on his introductions to community agencies in Madison, Wisconsin, Randy Stoecker convened a community conversation at the University of Wisconsin with agency directors interested in talking about their experience with service-learning. This led to student interviews with 67 agency directors in the Madison area as part of a graduate course in qualitative research methodologies, and eventually an edited book including chapters on the motivations of community organizations to host service learners, approaches to placing students and managing short-term time commitments, and challenges related to communication between faculty and the agencies entitled *The Unheard Voices: Community Organizations and Service Learning* (Stoecker & Tryon, 2009). Amy Mondloch, an agency director and contributor to the volume, describes the approach she and her colleagues take in working with service learners, which embodies her agency's motto: "everyone a learner, everyone a teacher, everyone a leader" (Mondloch, 2009, p. 137); she provides a wonderful orientation to the environment of nonprofit agencies for those who do not have direct experience, and wise advice for agency directors new to working with service learners. The salient point: there is much to consider by all partners before "opening the door" to service-learning (Mondloch, 2009, p. 138).

Too often university actors think of their activities as "doing for," rather than "doing with" the community (Ward & Wolf-Wendel, 2000; see also Bortolin, 2011; Sandy & Holland, 2006; Stoecker & Tryon, 2009). Thinking of service-learning as "doing for" reflects a charity-focused approach to civic engagement (Morton, 1995) and "emphasize[s] the position of privilege of campuses in relationship to their local communities" (Ward & Wolf-Wendel, 2000, p. 767). Such an attitude focuses on civic engagement as a desired outcome, rather than a process by which outcomes/changes are realized in the community. Encouraging a "doing with" approach is another way of advancing engagement as a process: civic engagement is "done with peers in the community, and from that service, new understanding and learning arises for all parties involved" (Ward & Wolf-Wendel, 2000, p. 777). Students who learn to identify problems and then work with the community to solve them may have a much greater likelihood of making meaningful contributions and continuing to participate in the processes of their community later in life (Bringle & Steinberg, 2010; Knapp et al., 2010).

In this chapter, community has been framed as a classroom, a place where college and university students learn discipline-specific concepts and civic aptitudes from university faculty and community members who are also nurturing students as active citizens. When community is framed in this way, the picture of community–university interaction that emerges emphasizes both private benefits to the individual student and public gains for communities. This image is somewhat different than current rhetoric positioning universities as primarily workforce training resources. Reimagining institutional purpose could support the shift from instrumental engagement to engagement as a process for interaction. The next step in advancing the shift to engagement-as-process should be a careful consideration of the potential contributions to be made by drawing on theoretical and pedagogical models that presume the educative value of interactions between community and university.

Directions for Future Research: Institutional Purpose

Throughout this monograph, I have insisted on three ideas as foundational for achieving the democratic possibilities of community–university interaction. First, the history, culture, and socioeconomic relations of the place where community–university interaction happens matter as much as what happens in that place (Cresswell, 2004; Harvey, 1993). A second key assumption reflects community development scholarship: overemphasis on economic development in communities may undermine development of community infrastructures, shift decision making away from community residents, and will likely further disadvantage members of already underrepresented groups (Barker & Brown, 2009; Bridger & Alter, 2006; Mathews, 2009; Reardon et al., 2009). Third, to ameliorate the marginalization of some residents, institutional leaders could adopt an engagement-as-process ethos, prioritizing relationship building over completing specific initiatives (Fear et al., 2006). Where communities are conceptualized as classrooms, making this shift requires rethinking institutional purpose and recommitting to higher education as a public good making a critical contribution to democratic processes and thereby to U.S. communities.

The literature reviewed in this chapter speaks to the efficacy of civic engagement in preparing students for their responsibilities as members of communities. Given the propensity of traditional processes to further disenfranchise already marginalized residents—especially the poor, people of color, those in rural areas, and the undereducated, the civic learning opportunities available to university students should prepare students not only to engage in community building but also to do so in a way that addresses existing patterns of disinvolvement by particular groups in communities. This is the point made by the participants in Sandy and Holland's (2006) study quoted above: through civic engagement, students should learn about others' experiences, because communities need these future policy makers and community leaders to have that knowledge.

Empirical findings support strongly the transformative potential of civic engagement in relation to student attitudes and propensity for future service. Even so, scholars continue to raise questions about the potential of service-learning to harm communities by perpetuating a view of need as deficiency and the possibility that short-term service-learning placements reinforce negative stereotypes, rather than changing attitudes (Eby, 1998; Holsapple, 2012). These concerns about the negatives of civic engagement should serve as impetus for further development of the pedagogy, rather than a rationale for discontinuing its use.

Place-based learning, and specifically a critical pedagogy of place, offers practical tools and constructs for university faculty committed to strengthening their civic-minded teaching practices. Place-based learning uses "the local community and environment as a starting point to teach . . . subjects across the curriculum" by "emphasizing hands-on, real-world learning experiences" (Sobel, 2004, p. 7). While place-based approaches would be very well suited to realizing the promise of community as a classroom, place-based educators do not necessarily ground their pedagogical practices in any critique of the power relations that shape a particular location. Cautionary tales about unbalanced interactions between community and university offered in this monograph suggest that such a critique of power is almost a prerequisite for changing the nature and outcomes of these interactions. In other words, place-based pedagogies alone may fall short of addressing the potential for further disenfranchising community residents from already marginalized groups. Critical theory, through its focused analysis of power, and the critical pedagogy tradition provide important conceptual links between the two traditions. The final section of this chapter considers each of these ideas in turn.

Place-Based Learning

Service-learning is one pedagogical expression of the larger community engagement movement at higher education institutions and, like all engagement activities, it is inherently place-based (Moore, 2013). Students participate in academically based service-learning and similar cocurricular civic activities offered at most U.S. colleges and universities. Civic engagement initiatives such as these are by definition place-based, in that they occur in specific geographically defined locations. The experiential learning opportunities themselves can be thought of as place-based learning because they foster pedagogical experiences that draw on students' lived experiences with local phenomena. Positioning the local community as a learning space and creating lesson plans focused on characteristics of the local environment, place-based learning is lauded by K–12 educators for producing student outcomes related to increased academic achievement, strengthened community ties, and commitment to active citizenship, as well as a heightened "appreciation for the natural world" (Sobel, 2004, p. 7). These outcomes mirror those called for by advocates of the university as a public good. Academic administrators and teaching faculty could support a shifting understanding of institutional purpose by translating place-based learning approaches to the university classroom.

The extant civic engagement literature provides examples of place-based learning adapted to a university course/setting. Smith (2002) outlines five overlapping categories of place-based approaches: culture studies, real-world problem solving, nature studies, internships and entrepreneurial opportunities, and induction into community processes. Through *culture studies,* students focus on "local cultural or historical phenomena directly related to [the students'] lives and the lives of people they know" (p. 588). After Hurricane Katrina, students in the Asian American Studies program at the University of Massachusetts at Boston traveled to New Orleans to volunteer in the relief effort specifically targeting New Orleans' Asian American community. For many students, this was the first meaningful connection they experienced with the culture and realities of daily lives in Asian American communities around the United States. Students explore the natural world through *nature studies* to learn about ecological issues facing their local community. For example, graduate students in chemistry at the University of Montana take advantage of university–industry partnerships to find research collaborations and funding through a local timber firm.

The Rural Entrepreneurship though Action Learning (REAL) Enterprises promotes *internships and entrepreneurial activities* in more than 30 states, partnering with high school, community college, and four-year institutions to identify unmet community economic development needs in local communities (http://www.ncreal.org). MBA students and business faculty at Winston-Salem State University have drawn on REAL resources to open a Center for Entrepreneurship. Initiatives like this center link to the growing emphasis at colleges and universities on fostering entrepreneurial efforts and small business growth as an important area of economic development, and students who participate in the related learning activities are also experiencing an *induction into community processes*, such as voting and community decision making. Business law faculty at Washington State University challenge students to identify and interview a local business leader who stood up for tolerance when such an act was unpopular or difficult. Students discuss these stories and consider their future opportunities to build inclusive communities.

Smith's (2002) work offers a schema for connecting course outcomes to community well-being and thereby, in the language of the civic engagement movement, for educating students for citizenship and participation in a democracy (Colby et al., 2007). Place-based approaches such as these provide students with powerful learning opportunities by presenting examples that demonstrate the more abstract principles addressed in many courses and texts. Place-based learning has also, however, been critiqued as overly identified with rural settings because of its affiliation with environmental education and other outdoor, experiential learning (Gruenewald, 2003). As a result, a place-based approach may seem irrelevant or inappropriate for implementation in urban settings, where many universities are located and where their students participate in civic engagement activities. Faculty in all institutional settings might choose to address this gap by drawing on the tools presented in critical theory, critical teaching practices/pedagogy, and a critical pedagogy of place.

Augmenting Place-Based Learning Through the Critical Theory Tradition

Two key ideas are fundamental to understanding the tools presented through a critical theory frame. First, power is the fundamental unit of analysis: who has it, how they use it, and to what end. Second, those who are marginalized in any society enjoy the possibility of resistance to that oppression. Critical theory positions "humans [as]. . . active agents of change" (Myers-Lipton, 1998, p. 246), and education as an important process for introducing individuals to their capacity to effect change in their surroundings (Brown, 2001).

Critical pedagogy, or teaching practices informed by critical theory, cultivates the disposition, knowledge, and skills necessary to activate change. For example, by developing critical literacy skills, a learner acquires the conceptual tools to read the world, first understanding the surface meaning of a word or a picture and then examining the deeper meanings of that word or image given the particular social context/power structure in which it is produced, and which has shaped the learner's perception of the word. The outcome of this critical literacy is the development of what Freire (1970) referred to as critical consciousness, or an awareness of the social forces/conditions impacting one's individual existence, typically in an oppressive or marginalizing sense (Rhoads, 2009). Freire's ideas have influenced the civic engagement movement for more than four decades, particularly related to course-based service-learning (Mitchell, 2008; Stenhouse & Jarrett, 2012).

Critical theorists have been particularly influential in shaping scholars' understanding of what students learn about power and how they come to acknowledge their capacity as change agents through civic engagement. Reporting on his meta-analysis of data from more than 400 interviews with student leaders across 10 years about eight different social activism initiatives in three countries, Rhoads (2009) highlights the importance of formal and informal civic engagement activities in supporting students' development of a critical consciousness, which will lead them to act and thereby embark on an iterative process of action, reflection, revised action aimed at making social change. Myers-Lipton (1998) supports the general contention that "when [encouraging students to question power relationships] is done through [civic engagement], students can become socialized to a new set of attitudes and values" (p. 256; Brown, 2001; Colby et al., 2007).

Critical pedagogy must consider place to empower students as change agents in the places they live (Gruenewald, 2003). Place-based pedagogies need not consider power dynamics in a place; however, given the potential for community–university interaction to exclude further some members of the community, these are crucial questions. The critical theory tradition offers theoretical tools to assist university administrators in examining power relations and effecting change in the community–university interaction. Through critical place-based learning approaches, students learn to ask questions about who sets the agenda for community–university interaction, and more importantly about who is involved, who is not, and how that might be changed.

A Critical Pedagogy of Place

Gruenewald (2003) brings critical pedagogy and place-based learning together in a critical pedagogy of place, challenging "all educators to reflect on the relationship between the kind of education they pursue and the kind of places we inhabit and leave behind for future generations" (p. 3). This author thinks of place in ecological terms, emphasizing human relationships and also the natural world. Still, his perspective is not incompatible with our focus on civic engagement and citizen action. Gruenewald also advances a model for research, theory, policy, and practice that explicitly shifts the focus of educational institutions, including colleges and universities, away from "individualistic and nationalistic competition in the global economy" (p. 3). This is another way of suggesting that universities ought not abandon their civic duties in favor of supporting economic growth over the well-being of all in the community.

Gruenewald's (2006) recommendations for curriculum reform linked to the Earth Charter offer questions that also point to the potential of a critical pedagogy of place to effect institutional and social change. He suggests that reformers begin by asking three questions: "What happened here in this place? What's happening here in this place? What should happen here in this place?" (p. 3). Community leaders must, he argues, understand the social, geographic, and historical contexts of their partnership, in addition to their project goals, before they can gauge "what works" in that setting (p. 3). To translate this into the language of engagement as process: when community and university representatives gather, they must first learn about the context of the proposed partners. They might ask about the history of the community or of specific interactions between the community and the university. Partners must also assess what is going on now, focusing attention on the current state of affairs in this neighborhood and identifying opportunities for collaboration. They identify goals for the collaboration by asking questions about what the community/neighborhood wants for the future. In short, partners must study and honor history, attend to current relationships, and develop a shared vision for their future. When university faculty, students, and professional staff participate in such activities, they are fulfilling their civic duty.

Those who position the system of higher education as a public good are arguing, in essence, that the purpose of colleges and universities is to serve the greater good through their roles as place makers, as educators, and as researchers or knowledge generators. In the process of connecting civic engagement to the curriculum, the service-learning movement has lost some of its commitment to the democratic purposes of education and to preparing students for citizenship (Saltmarsh & Hartley, 2011). The negative impact has been exacerbated by the typical/frequent conflating of citizenship and voting (e.g., Jacoby, 2006). Promoting a generic service-learning requirement will not address the disappearance of civic education: "The simple fact that the engagement takes place in the community context does not necessarily render that engagement *civic* in the full sense of the word" (Saltmarsh & Zlotkowski, 2011, p. 7). Saltmarsh (2005) has more to say on this point: civic engagement "is resulting in a technically improved teaching and learning method" but sometimes without intentional connections to civic learning outcomes (p. 28, as cited in Saltmarsh & Zlotkowski, 2011). The focus of the civic engagement movement must now be to "move beyond effective educational strategies like service-learning to learning outcomes that have a civic dimension" (p. 34, as cited in Saltmarsh & Zlotkowski, 2011). Teacher researchers and student affairs professionals can support this move by designing empirical research studies with implications for transforming policy and practice related to institutional purpose.

Methodologies to Transform Institutional Purpose

Higher education institutions are ideally positioned to cultivate civic-minded graduates who possess skills and dispositions for active citizenship (Bringle & Steinberg, 2010; Steinberg et al., 2011). Place-based learning approaches support the development of civic mindedness. Critical pedagogy assumes a particular approach to citizenship, emphasizing critical literacy skills and preparing individuals as agents of change. Adopting a critical pedagogy of place facilitates instructor efforts to foster a power-conscious civic-minded disposition that is vital for the preparation of citizens who take an inclusive approach to community building (Miller, 2008).

The work of preparing students along these lines falls primarily on the shoulders of university instructors and student affairs professionals. Teacher research, a tradition associated with common education, provides methodological tools for use in the university classroom and in other educational spaces such as student organizations and leadership initiatives. Teacher researchers focus on the relationships among teaching practices, learning outcomes, and other aspects of the student experience (Cochran-Smith & Lytle, 2009; Lankshear & Knobel, 2004). For example, instructors who utilize service-learning in their teaching commonly experience more negative teaching or course evaluations, with student comments focused on logistical difficulties, work load, and difficulties in seeing the relevance of the service to the course material (Beling, 2003). These student concerns represent tensions to be "mined" to generate research questions about the implementation of civic engagement activities, structuring intentional reflection activities, and partnering with community organizations to support service-learners (Shagoury & Power, 2012, p. 20).

Research conducted in learning spaces is common in the service-learning literature (see, e.g., Diaz & Perrault, 2010; Novick et al., 2011); few if any authors ground their scholarship in the teacher research tradition. Drawing on teacher research methodologies more intentionally focuses attention on teaching practice, facilitating evaluation of best practices as they are implemented in the new setting. This evaluation is critical given the limitations of place-based approaches which are embedded in the places where they occur, and as such should not be replicated elsewhere without careful consideration of the new place (Gruenewald, 2003; Smith, 2002).

Cochran-Smith and Lytle (2009), early contributors to the teacher research literature, now use the term *practitioner research* for this methodology, advocating its use by a broad range of educators in K–20 settings and community venues to contribute to educational reform. This methodological tradition also shows promise for advancing the necessary shift from engagement as product to engagement as process, particularly in this case by faculty and administrators acting as educators. Future research should also prioritize the involvement of student affairs practitioners, who educate through the cocurriculum. As mentors in living environments, advisors to student organizations, and academic advisors, they contribute significantly to the cognitive, psychosocial, and identity development of college students (Pascarella & Terenzini, 2005). As such, they also advance the development of power-conscious civic-minded graduates. Understanding more about how that happens in the informal learning spaces of living groups, student organizations, cocurricular leadership programs, and nonfaculty academic mentoring could support data-driven policies and practices needed in these settings to support learning objectives in the formal coursework.

The need to reconsider institutional purpose reflects the vital role played by colleges and universities in preparing graduates as active citizens. Building communities through democratic practices relies on community leaders who value the contributions of all residents and who prioritize inclusion. Preparing students for their roles as citizens in a diverse democracy is a long-held, widely agreed upon learning outcome of university education (Morse, 1989). In recent years, the importance of this outcome has been overshadowed by an emphasis on the college degree as primarily a private, economic benefit to individual degree holders with increased earning power. These two outcomes are not mutually exclusive; a university education can teach a graduate to value personal and also community economic and social well-being. Helping students to internalize these mutually reinforcing goals, and then to act accordingly will require university actors to make a conscious commitment to a new understanding of the purpose of a college education.

Community as Research Context

FACULTY HAVE TRADITIONALLY FULFILLED THREE ROLES: servant of the communities internal and external to their institution, teacher, and researcher (Jencks & Riesman, 1968). They contribute to the places, or communities, where they work through each of these roles. Faculty as public servants strengthen communities through formal and informal partnerships, consulting arrangements, and volunteer service. When they act as teachers, they advance academic, personal, and social/citizenship learning outcomes for students by incorporating civic engagement into curricular and cocurricular learning activities. The pioneers of the service-learning movement employed service-learning pedagogies, reflecting personal commitments to community well-being and, in many cases, to social change (Stanton et al., 1999). Faculty who pursue scholarly creative work or empirical research in the context of communities often do so out of a similar commitment to doing relevant, meaningful work (Giles, 2010; Moore & Ward, 2008, 2010). This chapter focuses on the work of faculty primarily at research universities in the United States who set community as the context for their scholarship. Ward (2003) tells the story of one such community-engaged teacher educator who volunteered with a local adult literacy program. Through her public service involvement with the program, this faculty member worked with organization leaders to identify service-learning opportunities for students in a reading methods course and also a line of research examining the adaptation of these methods for adult readers.

Much of the work of community–university engagement, particularly outside the economic development initiatives highlighted in the second chapter, is accomplished by individual faculty acting in their role as engaged scholar (Ward & Moore, 2010). Engaged scholarship differs from traditional scholarship in the engaged scholar's commitment to cocreating the knowledge required to address public issues (Glass & Fitzgerald, 2010). Beyond the value placed on reciprocity, all standards for rigor and reliability or trustworthiness apply (Glassick, Huber, & Maeroff, 1997). When community is positioned as a research site in this way, faculty are the primary university actors in community–university engagement. Issues related to faculty work, such as the quality of scholarship and faculty rewards policies, as well as the impact of this work on communities, are at the forefront of the discussion of community–university interaction in this chapter.

(Community-) Engaged Faculty Work

The early engaged scholars were primarily researchers in the social sciences and/or health-related fields (Driscoll & Lynton, 1999). Over 20 years, as faculty in a broader range of disciplines became involved in community-engaged research and scholarly activity, the array of activities and of community partners has expanded to include economic development, technology transfer, and consulting (e.g., Church, Zimmerman, Bargerstock, & Kenney, 2002/2003; Glass, Doberneck, & Schweitzer, 2011; Holland, Powell, Eng, & Drew, 2010). Still, faculty involvement in community-engaged research/scholarly activity primarily falls into two categories: community-based research and university–industry collaborations. Individual scholars participate in one or another of the two based on which approach best fits the unique combination of their academic field of study and personal commitments.

Community-Based Research

Community-based research (CBR) is a collaborative research strategy involving stakeholders in the research process, thereby democratizing knowledge by making it widely accessible (Strand, Marullo, Cutforth, Stoecker, & Donohue, 2003). Community leaders and/or citizens identify the problems and work with university researchers to design a study aimed at making social change. Community members, students, and university researchers are all recognized as experts on the research team, each bringing important experience and perspectives to the process. To the degree that university-based researchers engage with community stakeholders, CBR is also appropriately referred to as community-engaged research, so the two terms are used synonymously here.

Scholars and scholar–practitioners use CBR methodologies to investigate a broad range of research topics in the social and natural sciences, health-related fields, education, and the arts and humanities. The following examples are drawn from the peer-reviewed scholarship published in the top national journals of the community–university engagement movement. Some have been recognized by national organizations for excellence in engagement; they are all worthy examples of CBR projects, given their vetting in the scholarly peer review process. Beyond that standard, the partners in each project faced one or more issues typical in community-based research. The projects themselves are also excellent examples of the tight linkage between community–university partnerships and community-based research, which can—but does not always—occur within the context of formal partnership.

Water Quality and Wetlands Restoration. Sturgeon City, a 26-acre community green space and research facility on Wilson Bay near Jacksonville, North Carolina, operates through a civic-community–university partnership involving local municipal entities, state government departments, and area higher education institutions. Seventy years ago, area residents came to Wilson Bay to engage in a variety of water recreation activities; after the establishment of U.S. Marine Corps Base Camp Lejeune in Jacksonville in 1940, Onslow County's population increased 100-fold, and the area wastewater treatment facilities proved insufficient for the demand, contaminating the bay and leading to the decommissioning of several plants. Today, water quality scientists and graduate students from North Carolina State University and other area higher education institutions do community-based research at Sturgeon City, examining estuary water quality and the impact of human behavior on fish communities (e.g., Caldwell & Levine, 2009). Research findings support wetlands restoration and other initiatives to improve the health of the many aquatic species indigenous to this area.

The Association of Public and Land-Grant Universities recognized the Sturgeon City academic partnership with its top honor in 2010, the C. Peter Magrath Community Engagement Award (Levine, Hargett, McCann, Potts, & Pierce, 2011). The award recognizes four-year institutions for exemplary efforts to redesign their teaching, research, and public service/community engagement efforts to facilitate deepening engagement between the university and the community/region it serves. Sturgeon City is exemplary as a community–university partnership, such as those highlighted in the second chapter; the initiative is highlighted here, among examples of CBR research conducted by faculty, because it speaks to the power of community-based research to generate significant empirical findings that also have practical impact, in this case, on the economic, social, and environmental well-being of the place where the research is conducted.

Prevention and Treatment of Chronic Diseases. Minkler and Wallerstein (2003) recommend CBR models in public health that might include collaborations not only between academia and community members but also among other entities, including hospitals or county health departments. One such project, led by medical and public health researchers at the Center for Community-Based Research in the Dana-Farber Cancer Institute (DFCI), School of Public Health at Harvard University, includes a series of CBR projects. With the help of students, DFCI researchers recently piloted a low-cost intervention in community health centers in the Boston area, aimed at increasing cancer screening rates in these facilities. The current project is informed by a conceptual model based on findings from a previous CBR project. To design this intervention strategy, researchers reviewed findings from another earlier CBR study reflecting relationships among various individual and social factors and health behaviors, in the context of cancer screening and treatment (Sorenson et al., 2003). This example reinforces two points. CBR is an excellent approach for addressing complex issues deeply embedded in local culture, because, secondly, community members are valuable experts in navigating local culture and uncovering the implications of a particular study's findings.

CBR approaches are particularly prevalent in public health and medical research, as a result of three intertwined factors. One, urban health problems are typically complex, shaped as they are by characteristics of the particular health problem as well as local culture and individual behavior. Two, outside experts experience relatively little success in addressing elements of the problem that are shaped by the local culture. Three, and perhaps most importantly, community members want to play an active role, to partner with researchers in identifying and addressing the problems through authentic, community-based partnerships; they prefer the active participant role available to them on CBR research teams to the more passive, or one-way, community-placed expert outreach and/or research efforts (Minkler, 2005).

Educational and Community Outcomes in K–12 Schools. Universities can play a critical role in development efforts in impoverished communities, given the tremendous fiscal, physical, human, and knowledge resources at their disposal. University-assisted community schools (UACS), patterned on the work of the University of Pennsylvania Netter Center in West Philadelphia, demonstrate the potential for capitalizing on school–university–community partnerships to draw the fiscal, human, and knowledge resources of a university into redevelopment activities (Benson & Harkavy, 2000; Taylor, 2005). One such university-assisted community school, known as the Futures Academy, is located in the Fruit Belt neighborhood near downtown Buffalo, New York, and serves students from low-income neighborhoods across the city (Taylor & McGlynn, 2009, 2010). Graduate students affiliated with SUNY-Buffalo's Center for Urban Studies work with the Futures Academy teachers to offer the Community Classroom Program for sixth through eighth grade students. The Community Classroom Project (CCP) exists outside, but is complementary to, the school's standard curriculum, offering culturally relevant and place-based learning opportunities for students to realize their own capacity to make change in their community, a skill/disposition crucial to long-term community well-being (Taylor & McGlynn, 2010). Community-based researchers work within the parameters of the UACS partnership to examine topics such as the student cognitive and psychosocial outcomes associated with participation in the Futures Academy activities, and public school teacher willingness to cooperate and allow their students to be involved in the program, which takes time away from other instructional activities (Taylor & McGlynn, 2009, 2010).

The Arts and Humanities as Public Scholarship. Imagining America (IA) is a consortium of universities and organizations dedicated to advancing the public and civic purposes of humanities, arts, and design. Artists and scholars affiliated with IA include university faculty as well as community-based artists who work in conjunction with higher education institutions to build and enrich communities. Ellison and Eatman (2008) describe a variety of exemplar projects completed in recent years by IA members. In one such project advancing the public history of slavery, a Brown University historian has launched a research project exploring the university's role as a "site of conscience" (Ellison & Eatman, 2008, p. vi), resulting in a documentary film and curricular resources for teaching about the university's role in the current conversation about slavery. The Animating Democracy Initiative brought together university-based scholars and public artists to examine "who has voice and authority in critical writing about civically engaged art" (p. vi). Then, creative teams in three locations around United States engaged in dialogue about these issues and produced essays reflecting their conversations, which have been published along with commentary and responses from community collaborators (Atlas, Korza, Fiscella, & Bacon, 2005). The Kennesaw Mountain Writing Project, funded by the National Endowment for the Humanities, trained K–12 teachers for community-engaged research and teaching. The teacher partners took on public scholar roles, investigating and writing about their home regions, and then used their findings to inform place-based curriculum materials to engage students in their communities.

Participation Processes in Community Revitalization. Scholars in studio-based fields such as urban planning and architecture, as well as community development and regional studies, also frequently use CBR methods, answering research questions about the processes of community building and the definition/use of public space. González, Sarmiento, Urzua, and Luévano (2012) conducted a case study of a community revitalization effort in Santa Ana, California's Logan and Lacey neighborhoods from 2007 through 2012. The authors are faculty members at three universities in the area. However, they got involved in this project because of their personal connections to the area. All three grew up either in the Logan or the Lacey neighborhood, and members of their families still live there. In examining this project, we learn more about the experiences of faculty who pursue community-based or community-engaged scholarship as a path for enacting their own values and social commitments (Peters, Alter, & Schwartzbach, 2010).

In this particular case, city leaders and developers intended the Station District project to revitalize 94 acres in downtown Santa Ana. Discussions about improving the condition of these neighborhoods have been ongoing for more than 40 years. Resident participation had previously been somewhat limited, in many instances by design on the part of city leaders. This time, though, neighborhood leaders pushed for and won a place in the planning conversations. González et al. (2012) analyzed archival documents and their own notes from coalition meetings, public forums, and official minutes from city council meetings to create a map of the process by which the community coalition, city officials, and the developer reached agreement on plans to preserve the historic and cultural identity of the area. In their analysis of this data set, the authors differentiate between experienced, "grasstips" community activists and "grassroots" residents of the local community with no organizing experience (p. 233). This distinction is an important one to note in this project for two reasons. First, the distinction explains why, in Santa Ana, previous efforts to solicit public input still resulted in development plans that were detrimental to existing neighborhoods. More importantly, though, this story of the Santa Ana Collaborative for Responsible Development (SA-CReD) highlights the need to provide for wide participation and provides an example of one community's efforts to interrupt the tendency to exclude the less experienced from important conversations about the future of the place where they live.

Community-based research happens both within and outside partnerships such as those described in the second chapter. The examples presented above reflect CBR projects embedded in existing community–university partnerships, as well as those established by individual (or small groups of) faculty in the context of a community coalition. The difference between the two sets of examples is somewhat nuanced. Partnerships such as the one between Arizona State University and the city of Phoenix resulting in a new downtown campus prioritized the university's capacity to contribute to the revitalization of the urban core. An economic development partnership has also developed around Sturgeon City, involving multiple local universities and municipal entities, as well as a U.S. military installation. That complex infrastructure of relationships and projects began with one faculty member at North Carolina State University working with the State Department of Marine Fisheries to explore water quality issues affecting the coastal fishing industry. Public scholars and their scholarship recognized by IA rarely involve institutional commitment to the partnership beyond the time and effort of individual faculty members and their students. The same can be said of González et al.'s (2012) involvement in Santa Ana city planning. In some instances, such as the university-assisted schools' initiatives and public health research, more formal administrative structures such as a center or an institute do exist within the institution. Other faculty pursue their personal commitments and research interests more independently.

These examples of community-based research and public scholarship all emerge from a commitment to the university as an important resource to ensure strength and vitality of community infrastructure and community residents. This discourse is much less evident in the last 15 years, replaced by talk about ways in which universities can support the economic growth of individual communities, regions, and the United States. University–industry collaborations, a distinct kind of community–university partnership focused on monetizing research or other economic activity, are fraught with a variety of challenges and provide additional opportunities to reflect on issues related to institutional culture and faculty work, particularly for faculty in STEM and business fields.

University–Industry Collaborations
Beginning in the late 1970s, the U.S. government and corporate leaders looked increasingly to higher education institutions and academic researchers for technological innovations that would win the global economic competition with Japan. Technology transfer mechanisms, such as university–industry partnerships, collaborative research, joint publication with industry colleagues, joint supervision of graduate students, and faculty consulting, connect individual academics with industry partners. In 2005, 52% of

scientists responding to a survey by Link, Siegel, and Bozeman (2007) reported involvement in work of some sort with industry colleagues, including technology transfer activities, joint publication of research, and academic consulting.

Even as participation expands, "scientists view university-industry research relationships in complex and conflicting ways" (Welsh, Glenna, Lacy, & Biscotti, 2008, p. 1863). One group of biomedical scientists referred to relationships with the pharmaceutical industry as "dancing with a porcupine" (Lewis et al., 2001, p. 783). Those who favor collaboration and entrepreneurial behavior cite resulting boosts to economic well-being and sharing of knowledge from these activities. Others express concern about restrictions on the flow of knowledge, and also a general reduction in research productivity, when research becomes proprietary. Critics' concerns seem to be somewhat unfounded. The most common motivation to engage with industry, endorsed by 74.5% of physical and engineering science faculty surveyed by D'Este and Perkmann (2011), was to expand the applicability of their own research. Thursby and Thursby's (2011) analysis of a database of research disclosure at eight U.S. universities between 1983 and 1999 suggested that commercial appeal did not subvert faculty interests in basic research, nor did traditional measures of productivity, such as the citation index used in this study, show any decline. Rather, the authors' findings suggest that "both basic and applied research is greater when faculty can benefit from commercialization of their research effort" (Thursby & Thursby, 2011, p. 1077). This may be the case because applied research requires greater "partner interdependence" and therein "enables exploratory learning by academics, leading to new ideas and projects" (Perkmann & Walsh, 2009, p. 1033).

As in the earlier discussion of community-based research, these examples reflect the current scholarly discussion of this area of faculty research, highlighting issues raised by critics and supporters of university–industry collaboration. Exactly the elements that are most concerning to some are used by others to support the promise of university–industry collaborations, based on Welsh et al.'s (2008) survey exploring the attitudes of biological sciences faculty at nine research universities about changes in policies regarding university–industry research relationships. Effective intellectual property policies can facilitate interaction with industry scientists at the same time that it restricts communication in the scientific community, limiting the contribution of science to the public good. Strong concerns on these points are evident in the higher education literature, suggesting the continued salience of tensions between the public and private purposes of higher education as they relate to faculty scholarly activity (Mendoza, 2012; Slaughter & Leslie, 1997; Slaughter & Rhoades, 2004; Welsh et al., 2008). Nonetheless, what Mendoza (2012) terms "industry-friendly department[s]" are increasingly common, particularly at major research universities where the collaborations provide welcome funding for faculty research, as well as support for graduate students and opportunities for these students to work in industry settings.

The deciding factor in a department's attitude toward university–industry collaboration appears to be the disciplinary and institutional contexts in which the department exists (Mendoza, 2012). Differences based on academic discipline have, however, been largely ignored in the literature on academic capitalism, and inappropriately so, Mendoza argues. Academic discipline together with specific institutional context influence significantly the culture and norms of a particular department. The effect of these layers is not, however, cumulative, given the likelihood that "each . . . context . . . experience[s] and view[s] industry-academia collaborations differently" (Mendoza, 2012, p. 27). To demonstrate the salience of each of these contexts, Mendoza presents a case study of Industry-Friendly department, described as a "have" (rather than a "have not") among departments at this particular institution. This science and engineering unit is housed in a $50-million-state-of-the-art research facility with glass walls and trendy furniture in the chair's office, and differences in office space and lab facilities among faculty within the same department as visual cues to who was, or was not, involved in industry collaborations. Mendoza ultimately makes an important point: there is no longer any point in asking whether or not collaborations should exist between academic and industry-based scientists, she writes, given that these relationships are necessary in many disciplines. Instead, the conversation now must focus— as this monograph does at a metalevel—on addressing the issues that arise in these relationships, such as disparity of resources among faculty in the same department depending on involvement in industry collaboration, open communication of and about scientific results, and intellectual property rights.

This case study highlights two significant things about university–industry collaborations as one type of engaged scholarship. First, industry collaborations are also excellent examples of university researchers' efforts to produce relevant knowledge that will improve practice. Technology transfer activities such as these make important contributions to the nation's economic competitiveness and community well-being. Second, through collaborations, scientists connect directly with industry partners who use knowledge at least partially produced in the academy to solve problems impacting communities, regions, and the United States as a whole.

The two types of community-engaged scholarship discussed in this section—community-based research and university–industry collaborations—link university faculty/researchers to communities through tangible relationships within and also outside formal partnerships. Community is framed as the context within which this research occurs; when community is understood as research context, or laboratory, the implications of a given study are more clearly connected to the effect of the scholarship on residents of the community and the community infrastructure itself, and individual residents. Taking this approach keeps the researcher's focus on solving practical problems, and in this way faculty contribute to the quality of life and economic strength of communities. However, when engagement is viewed simply as an instrumental goal or outcome, rather than a process by which the partners interact, every stage of the research is compromised from the perspective of ensuring mutuality and reciprocity. The problem might be defined from a textbook rather than lived experience. Research questions focus the study on academic issues rather than the real-life challenges that most need clarification. Community members could be token representatives rather than active, valued members of the research team, participating appropriately in the data collection and analysis and receiving the training they need to contribute to the process. Most importantly, the interpretation of the findings, and coming to understand their significance, suffers without the community members' assistance to contextualize the findings, grounding them in the historical, social, and cultural realities of the place where the engagement is occurring.

The Impact of Engaged Faculty Work on Communities

Critics both within and outside the academy argue that issues related to the community's experience of engaged research continue to receive insufficient attention (Afshar, 2005; Stoecker et al., 2010), given the centrality of the community and the espoused desire of university leaders to impact communities. Universities are expected by many different constituents to engage with their communities, and they do so through organized initiatives and individual action. Some of these collaborations transform communities and generate important new knowledge in a discipline; others do not. Those that do not produce such transformative results may fail to achieve their goals because true collaborations were not established, and the group did not prioritize reciprocity and mutual benefit (Anyon & Fernández, 2007). Community members speak eloquently about their experiences and frustrations with university initiatives that are too often "community-placed," rather than "community-based" (Minkler, 2005, p. ii3). Scholar–practitioners acknowledge structural and cultural issues that inhibit individuals and institutions from developing truly collaborative relationships. In this section, I consider both perspectives.

Community Experiences With Engaged Scholarship

A community representative attending a national gathering of community leaders and their university partners shared with other attendees his previous experiences partnering with university faculty. Glenn (a pseudonym assigned by Pasque, 2010) expressed his frustration at the many times he or another community organization representative had been invited (i.e., required) to present "a dog and pony show" to educate university representatives about the situation in the community and/or the work of the agency (Pasque, 2010, pp. 295–296). He continued, calling instead for more open dialogue between university and community organizations about "what we're wrestling with, . . . what we're failing against, . . . [and what] we're trying to do differently. *[T]hen,*" he says, "we can begin to talk about what needs to be done together" (emphasis in the original; Pasque, 2010, p. 295).

The John W. Gardner Center for Youth and Their Communities at Stanford University partnered with San Francisco Bay area community organizations to advance community–youth development (Anyon & Fernández, 2007). Before staff of the Gardner Center could work effectively with their partners, they first needed to address negative images of the university held by local residents. Three issues created mistrust in the partners' relationships, in particular among members of low-income communities: researchers in previous collaborations made little to no effort to learn from residents; prioritized their own research agendas over community needs; and planned for the work as if it were a short-term project rather than a long-term relationship.

Glenn and his San Francisco counterparts point toward the central issue in the critique of community as research context: the failure of (many) university actors to dedicate necessary time and attention to relationship building as a foundation for successful community–university interactions (Fear et al., 2006). Many other scholars have written on this topic, highlighting structural and cultural issues within higher education institutions, challenges inherent in the organization of and socialization to faculty work, faculty rewards systems and the "pursuit of prestige" (O'Meara, 2007, p. 122; see also Holland & Gelmon, 1998), and "the continuing bias of institutional civic engagement programs toward serving their own goals, rather than those of the community" (Stoecker et al., 2010, p. 180).

Evaluating the Impact of University Actions

Regardless of the specific approach taken to address an issue, or establish a relationship, higher education institutions have a poor record in evaluating the impact of their civic engagement initiatives, whether formal partnerships such as those in the second chapter, or the faculty research projects explored earlier in this chapter. The underlying causes for the poor record across institutions include characteristics of the particular institution, particularly its faculty rewards system, and of the individual faculty themselves, making this an issue that must be considered here in the discussion of engaged faculty work (Stoecker et al., 2010).

First, universities are primarily focused on student learning outcomes, and second, manuscripts/publications are typically written soon after the project is "finished," meaning that there is not adequate time to examine impact/outcomes. The scholarly literature is also to blame to some extent, given that the theories informing civic engagement initiatives do not, typically, emphasize community change, and engagement professionals and faculty are typically unfamiliar with the literature that would address this topic. These factors keep academics focused on outputs (e.g., the number of people participating in the stream restoration project) rather than outcomes (e.g., the increase in the number of aquatic species in the stream over three years; Stoecker et al., 2010, pp. 180–183).

Faculty allocate their time to those activities for which they are rewarded (Fairweather, 1996). At present, many universities reward faculty through a system of tenure and promotion, salary increases, awards, and other campus-specific initiatives. Faculty who complete (more of) the most valued activities, whatever those are, are promoted, or receive higher compensation, or benefit more from specific initiatives such as special funding opportunities. Because this is the system in which they will be working, future faculty members are also socialized to operate in this kind of environment, one which prioritizes publications and securing grant funding over relationship building; socialization of new faculty to old norms makes changing the existing approach difficult (O'Meara, 2008; O'Meara & Jaeger, 2006). The result will likely be a continued failure to adjust faculty culture in such a way to foster an engagement-as-process ethos on a particular campus.

Pasque's (2010) participant, Glenn, calls for more dialogue between universities and communities about "what needs to be done together" (p. 295). In this phrase, he offers another way to say that collaborators need to start by building a relationship. Trust is also crucial to successful engagement (Larson & McQuiston, 2012). Throughout this monograph, I have called repeatedly for institutions, their leaders, and other representatives to rethink engagement, to adopt and then enact a new ethos, one that prioritizes relationship building. Where faculty work is concerned, academic administrators can prioritize building stable networks of partners to encourage senior faculty to integrate their junior colleagues into their work. Faculty can work through these networks to identify issues and resources within the community, as well as tap into university resources to support community-driven change efforts. The first step will be to recognize the time-/labor-intensive project as critical and then to reward faculty for the steps they take toward realizing this new idea.

Encouraging Engaged Scholarship

Faculty rewards systems at most institutions—particularly where promotion and tenure are concerned—still reflect the traditional emphasis on research over teaching, and offer only a token acknowledgement of service (Jaeger & Thornton, 2005; O'Meara, 2002, 2010; Ward, 2003). The implicit emphasis on extramural funding and peer-reviewed publications—and in turn, the time faculty allocate to this work—often poses a related second barrier to pursuing engaged scholarship. Building authentic relationships with community members and organizations is critical to the work of community–university partnerships and engaged scholarship. Relationship building of this sort is, like research and writing for publication, time intensive, and the two activities often compete with one another for a scholar's time and attention. Untenured faculty are regularly counseled to give priority to research activities until they earn tenure, particularly at institutions where community-engaged scholarship is not valued on par with more traditional forms of research productivity (Austin & McDaniels, 2006; O'Meara & Jaeger, 2006).

Anticipating this challenge, Glassick et al. (1997) offered the first resource for evaluating each of the four domains of scholarship in *Scholarship Assessed*, intended as a companion volume for Boyer's (1990) *Scholarship Reconsidered: Priorities of the Professoriate*. The authors outlined standards for scholarly work and made recommendations for documenting engaged scholarship. Driscoll and Lynton (1999) provided 16 prototype portfolios as examples of documentation approaches emphasizing the presentation of faculty work as an integration of teaching, research, and service. Ellison and Eatman (2008), on behalf of IA, have provided a guide to documenting and evaluating public, or engaged, scholarship in the arts and humanities. Imagining America's Assessing Practices in Public Scholarship Research Group has recently released its first two case studies offered as examples of public scholarship and of documenting the work for promotion and tenure. Scholars have also provided stories from extension educators, and faculty integrating teaching, research, and service (Moore & Ward, 2010), as well as specific examination of how these faculty have documented their work for promotion and tenure (Moore & Ward, 2008, 2010; Peters, Jordan, Adamek, & Alter, 2005; Peters et al., 2010).

Individual campuses also turned attention to effecting policy change to support individual engaged faculty. Many revised their promotion and tenure documents to reflect an expanded definition of scholarship and to recognize engaged scholarship on par with more traditional examples of research (Hyman et al., 2001/2002; O'Meara & Rice, 2005). More recently, Saltmarsh, Giles, et al. (2009) examined the extent to which institutions applying for Carnegie Foundation Community Engagement classification in 2006 had reshaped faculty reward policies. In 2006, 33 of the 57 applications reviewed for Carnegie Foundation Community Engagement classification provided information on promotion and tenure guides. Half of those included community-engaged scholarship in their revised guidelines, yet only nine campuses have "Boyerized guidelines" (p. 15). Only three of those reflect a change in language to specifically address community engagement; for example, one of these institutions defines scholarship to include "'community-based research, technical assistance, demonstration projects, impact assessment, and policy analysis,' as well as 'scholarly work relating to the study or promotion of public engagement'" (as cited by Saltmarsh, Giles, et al., 2009, p. 16). While engagement with the community is most typically categorized as service ($n = 11$), eight institutions include policies that reflect an understanding of engagement as an integration of research, teaching, and service.

Realigning the Institutional Economy

"Effective community engagement requires steady, long-term relations" and very likely also a shift in what is valued by the university (Maurrasse, 2010 p. 228). Although much emphasis is put in that direction, the dynamic tension between scholarship and engagement is not completely a matter to be addressed in the promotion and tenure system. O'Meara (2010) suggests that the focus on promotion and tenure policies is too narrow; it may indeed miss the point of the discussion given the need for institutional change, and furthermore, to support more proactively the establishment of mutually beneficial relationships with community members (Butin, 2003, 2006; Saltmarsh, Giles, et al., 2009; Weerts & Sandmann, 2008). A faculty rewards system, O'Meara's (2010) argument goes, is a larger thing which should be understood as informing both the individual tenure and promotion policies that support or hamper engagement, as well as shape the way faculty and administrators think about or the degree to which they value community engagement, which would in turn be reflected in the way the policies are enacted. Tenure and promotion polices are different than, but reflective of, the rewards system itself:

a reward system should be considered not only in terms of the formal and structural policies in place but as a more complex set of interacting social, cultural, political, and economic factors that encourage some behaviors over others. . . . Reward systems are shaping how faculty present and understand their work. Also, rewards systems are an important cultural and symbolic way departments, colleges and institutions say what matters. (p. 272)

Further, she argued, administrators who overlook the value of engaged scholarship miss important opportunities to capitalize on what individual faculty can contribute to the institution: "each person. . . brings with them certain currencies . . . to offer" to a particular department or college; understanding individual efforts as part of the whole, "[t]he prestige one faculty member offers through peer-reviewed journals may be considered equal to the currency of a new engagement-oriented NSF grant or outstanding teaching award, depending on the institutional economy at the time" (O'Meara, 2010, p. 277). The evaluation systems for reward and recognition and for faculty development must, accordingly, give proper and weighted consideration to contributions in research, teaching, and service, being very careful not to isolate these work roles as separate endeavors when establishing faculty evaluation and reward processes. This kind of evaluation system will also pay great dividends for the communities served.

Regardless of how one envisions this new reward system, some basic changes need to be achieved. First, recognizing that faculty are often the principle actors of the engagement movement, institutional leadership must go into the endeavor understanding that achieving an engagement ethos will require rewarding faculty for engaged teaching, scholarship, and service. Many institutions have changed their rewards policy, or "Boyer-ized" it as we read earlier. "Boyer-ized" policies are those that have been brought into alignment with Ernest Boyer's (1990, 1996) expanded definitions of scholarship recognizing discovery, application, integration, teaching and learning, and engagement all as scholarly activities (e.g., see Hyman, et al., 2001/2002, for a discussion of the UniSCOPE model developed at Penn State University; Saltmarsh et al., 2009). Scholars are beginning to think about what might be entailed in realigning the institutional economy. These processes can be used to shift the focus on individual campuses from engagement as a desired outcome to engagement as a process. Making this change is a matter of changing institutional culture more so than anything else, given that revised policies are still carried out by individuals. The key then is to change not what activities are counted as engagement but instead to change the culture around engagement, by considering what institutions value in terms of how, with whom, and to what end university actors engage with members of the community they serve.

Directions for Future Research: Institutional Culture

The values expressed through an institution's promotion and tenure documents and in the evaluation of one's scholarship communicate the culture of a particular institution, as do the attitudes of those at the institution on issues of expertise, and who might be considered an expert (Tierney, 1988). Given the well-documented barriers to engaged scholarship presented by the faculty rewards system and the devaluing of practice-based knowledge by the academy, changes in institutional culture are in order to support a transition to engagement as a process for building and sustaining relationships between universities and the communities they serve.

Academics are socialized through dominant doctoral education models and campus cultures into the role of *expert* (Holland & Gelmon, 1998; McDowell, 2001). In the political arena, expert knowledge sometimes "replaces a political decision. Often if 'experts' can be said to agree, political debate is closed down or even pre-empted" (Edkins, 2005, p. 65). Contextualized in the local community, Edkins's comments point to the problems inherent in positioning academics as *experts* in community–university engagement: their involvement can easily be used to preempt citizen input, as in González et al.'s (2012) description of revitalization efforts in Santa Rosa offered earlier in this chapter, where residents had been excluded from the planning process, sometimes by design, for almost 40 years.

Many argue that society's problems are too complex to be adequately addressed by citizens who, according to opinion polls, are too ignorant and/or uninterested to make worthwhile contributions (Barker & Brown, 2009; Fischer, 2000, 2009). Following this line of thinking, despite the dangers of disenfranchising the public, experts are necessary precisely because of what they know how to do. Policy expert Fischer (2000) disagrees: "[C]itizens . . . are much more capable of grappling with complex problems than generally assumed" (p. 32). The implication for him is clear: "Solutions to many complex problems are found through more, rather than less, interaction between citizens and experts" (p. 33). Achieving Fischer's goal in the context of community–university partnerships will require a better understanding of how power works in relationships among citizens and university-based experts (Saltmarsh, Hartley, & Clayton, 2009; Sandmann, Kliewer, Kim, & Omerikwa, 2010).

Future researchers would be wise to query such phenomena as defining expertise within the context of community–university partnerships, identifying experts, and understanding how who we acknowledge as expert has the effect of excluding others considered nonexpert. Postcolonial theory, with its focus on relationships between dominant and marginalized groups within a particular community/society, provides constructs potentially useful for exploring power dynamics inherent in the interactions of community and university representatives within community–university partnerships.

Where Expertise Empowers: Postcolonial Theory

Postcolonial writers theorize a dominant group's use of power to shape social norms and values and thereby the experience of those who do not have access to such power. Postcolonial theorists use notions of *colonizer* (at the center, having access to power) and *colonized* (on the periphery, marginalized and without access) to understand the ways in which people indigenous to a particular place are forced into identities and social positions dictated by outsiders. Viewing the common language of community–university interaction through a postcolonial lens highlights implicit assumptions that are potentially problematic for achieving the shift to engagement as a process and advancing democratic participation in communities:

> *Talking of the center and periphery recalls several common phrases in the engagement lexicon, including* university and community, researcher and community partner, *and* town and gown. *Through such terminology, academics position communities and community leaders as peripheral in a geographic sense, and potentially marginal in the activity of community-university engagement. (Sandmann, Moore, & Quinn, 2012, p. 29)*

This passage highlights the pervasive use of terms in engagement that reinforce distinctions between those with access to power and those without. Possessing expertise, or particularly valued knowledge and skills, is also a form of power in that experts sometimes use their expertise to shape social norms and values, and following the definition of postcolonial theory above, thereby influence the experiences of others.

Scholar–practitioners might draw on postcolonial theory to explore issues such as these fruitfully, bringing attention to power structures that marginalize individuals and/or groups in partnerships. Sandmann et al. (2012) argue for postcolonial theory as a tool for increasing reciprocity between community and university by highlighting areas of concern in a partnership more so than offering specific strategies for addressing the concerns. Seeing community-university partnerships as a contribution to deliberative democracy and as a venue within which deliberative practices might be used to explore, for example, the implications of community-engaged research or to develop research-informed recommendations may address some of the limitations of postcolonial theory as a tool for engaged scholars.

Where Expertise Excludes: Deliberative Democracy

Conflicts among individuals or groups with like values are typically addressed through voting or other approaches associated with participatory democracy (Hanson & Howe, 2011). Such an adversarial approach to resolving community-level issues seems almost doomed to fall short of finding a solution. Carcasson and Sprain (2012) suggest an alternative to aggregative practices such as voting or expert decision making: deliberative politics. Citizens address a community issue through facilitated dialogue designed to elicit multiple points of view and then as a group evaluate options for resolving the situation. Indeed, the very complex problems facing communities make it critical for communities to "develop and sustain their capacity for deliberative democracy and collaborative problem solving through the high quality interactive communication across perspectives fostered by deliberative democracy" (Carcasson & Sprain, 2012, p. 15).

Faculty acting in their roles as researchers can support deliberative practices. In fact, they are uniquely well suited to do so, given the "wicked," or complex, nature of social problems currently facing U.S. communities (Carcasson & Sprain, 2012). Wicked problems cannot be clearly defined and do not have definitive right answers. Each one is a symptom of another, and they are all unique because of the context in which they occur. How the problem is framed determines how it might be addressed, and the framing reflects the complex interplay of diverse personal values (Rittel & Webber, 1973). They are the hallmark of diverse democracies. Wicked problems are not solved. Rather, citizens negotiate tradeoffs among the competing values represented within their community. Deliberative decision making can be facilitated by impartial parties, and it can be informed by empirical research and evidence-based promising practices (Carcasson & Sprain, 2012, pp. 16-18).

University-based researchers could serve as facilitators and/or information resources.

Critics of deliberative democratic models cite human nature, lack of individual civic capacity, and the possibility that civic action can lead just as easily to exclusion and social fragmentation as to democratic outcomes. History bears out this observation: in the United States after World War II, members of antidesegregation organizations led civic activities aimed specifically at threatening the personal safety of and disenfranchising a large segment of the U.S. population (Armony, 2004). Lefrançois and Ethier (2010) also acknowledge the gap between the ideal of deliberative democracy and the reality of 21st century aggregative politics; however, they argue that the gap is neither static nor permanent and that it can be narrowed over time. Individual faculty and institutional leaders interested in working toward deliberative democracy may be able to do so by embracing engagement-as-process as it is outlined in this monograph.

Most issues currently facing the world's communities will be resolved by citizens working with each other to negotiate the wicked problems facing their communities (Cruz, 2007). University-based researchers will make very important contributions to community-based problem solving, once the exact nature of the problem is clear, because established scientific processes, community collaboration models, new technologies, and other areas of faculty expertise will almost certainly be useful in moving forward. Accepting this new reality effects a cultural change and new ways of thinking about faculty: as resources rather than experts, on the periphery rather than at the center of community processes.

Methodologies to Explore Institutional Culture

Engagement-as-process presumes university-based scholars acting as supports for community-led change. This is not a new idea in the scholarship related to community–university interaction (Dzur, 2008; Sullivan, 2005); it is, however, one that has been underexamined, given the pervasive emphasis on engagement as a desired product or outcome. Future research is needed: empirical studies aimed at understanding how community leaders and university administrators and/or faculty partners, what is needed from each party when these collaborations take place, and how universities and community organizations can support them.

Faculty doing community-engaged scholarship, and scholars writing about community–university interaction can contribute to our understanding of these issues through participatory inquiry and/or case study methodology. Single-site case studies would illuminate the experience of one community addressing one issue, but tell us relatively little about the broader phenomenon of university participation in deliberative democracy, or faculty working as resources. Multisite case studies, allowing for cross-case comparison, could address these limitations quite effectively by providing insight as to appropriate/necessary adaptation of the model to fit a particular place. Using narrative methodologies, other scholars might collect stories from faculty about their work as resources, or making the shift from expert to resource orientation.

The basic premise underlying this view of faculty as resource is straightforward: those who have lived experience of the various issues facing U.S. communities should, through deliberative processes, identify the values that matter most to them and use those to name or define the problem(s) facing the place where they live. Those who are most directly impacted by the solution should drive the process of change. The role of the university-based expert in a deliberative process is not to lead but to assist by helping to build the capacity of the community's leaders (Carcasson & Sprain, 2012; Mathews, 2009).

Adopting engagement-as-practice complements this new conceptualization of faculty as resources. Ironically, making the shift from engagement-as-product to engagement-as-process is itself a wicked problem to which there is no clear solution. In previous chapters, I have isolated characteristics of the problem and offered theoretical and methodological suggestions for advancing the scholarship related to these issues. The findings from such studies will provide important information to inform policy and practice for current faculty and academic administrators.

The implications of these findings, like those from studies suggested in previous chapters, have the potential to be wide-ranging, impacting universities as well as the communities they serve. In the following chapter, after summarizing the key arguments made in this monograph, I offer recommendations. Some of these originate in published literature while others emerge from the discussion of the varieties of community–university interaction highlighted by asking about how different definitions of community produce the terms, and the outcomes, of community–university engagement.

Implications and Recommendations

IN THE 20th CENTURY, terms like *scholar* and *researcher* invoked a stereotypical image dating from the Cold War of scientists in an ivory tower toiling away to answer questions of basic science, of interest simply because the answer remained unknown rather than because the answer might have some usefulness when applied to a real-world problem (Cox, 2010). Boyer (1990) pushed institutional leaders to broaden the definition of scholarship emphasizing not only traditional discovery as a scholarly endeavor but also application, teaching and learning, and the integration of knowledge. Stokes (1997) suggested a new paradigm, calling university researchers to work in Pasteur's Quadrant, where the search for foundational knowledge explores questions inspired by problems of use. In this new environment, many faculty evolved into engaged scholars (Glass & Fitzgerald, 2010), connecting their teaching, research, and public service directly to realities faced by individuals and communities. Engaged faculty work represents a manifestation of the university's renewed commitment to a civic mission.

The work of Ernest Boyer, Donald Stokes, and others provided a new vocabulary for articulating the values and purposes of faculty work. The intransigent nature of academic culture, and of disciplinary norms (Becher & Trowler, 2001; Saltmarsh, Giles, et al., 2009), has, however, stymied the ability of engaged scholars and administrators using the new language to bring about a new reality at a systemic level, as evidenced by the continued dominance of traditional definitions of scholarship in most institutions' faculty rewards policies (O'Meara, 2005, 2010). In effect, then, the *Boyerization* (Saltmarsh, Giles, et al., 2009) of the faculty work discourse may have simply given us new names for, and a few new ideas about the relationship among, the tripartite faculty roles outlined by Jencks and Riesman (1968) nearly 50 years ago. Seeing community cast in three different roles, as I have done in this monograph, does not address these issues, which are internal and arguably idiosyncratic to the academy. Rather, these frames focus the conversation in three areas: institutional culture, institutional purpose, and institutional change.

Understanding community as research context points to elements of institutional culture that complicate the necessary change processes. The professional assistance/outreach model positions community members as somewhat ignorant, and in doing so threatens the quality/success of community–university partnerships and—in particular—community-engaged research. Grappling with the impact of entering into relationships that are based on the assumption that *we* know more than *them*, and *we* are here to *help them*, has been shown, repeatedly, to be problematic in various modalities of community–university interaction, including service-learning and engaged research. Community members are important teachers in the service-learning experience (Sandy & Holland, 2006; Stoecker & Tryon, 2009; Worrall, 2007) as well as critical participants in policy development (Fischer, 2000) and public deliberations (Fischer, 2009; Mathews, 2009).

Conceptualizing community as classroom points to the need to revisit questions of institutional purpose. Higher education institutions are ideally positioned to used place-based teaching approaches to cultivate civic-minded graduates (Bringle & Steinberg, 2010; Steinberg et al., 2011) who possess the skills and dispositions required for participation in a deliberative democracy. Universities are also inherently well suited to adopt an organizational learning stance (Boyce, 2003; Kezar, 2005b); indeed, they must do so to sustain the organizational changes necessary to operationalize a new way of relating with nonacademic peers (Boyce, 2003).

Positioning community as historical/cultural/social place highlights the need for changes in the way that universities typically operate (Hodges & Dubb, 2012). Connecting engagement to the need for institutional change has been a ubiquitous recommendation in the scholarship related to all varieties of community–university interaction for decades, beginning with the earliest writings urging universities to set new priorities emphasizing community–university interaction, and outlining changes that might be necessary in the way universities operate to realize these new priorities (Lynton & Elman, 1987; Saltmarsh & Hartley, 2011). Colleges and universities enacting an anchor institution mission will, for example, need to learn to work in underresourced communities (Hodges & Dubb, 2012). This will be an organizational learning challenge, and it will also be a personal learning opportunity for individual institutional actors, who will likely have to engage in "courageous learning about race, self, community, and social action" (Cain, 2012, p. 201) to become the people they need to be to do this work.

Recommendations for Realizing the Civic Imperative of Higher Education

How individual actors in community–university interactions think about community influence their interactions, and ultimately shape the structure and outcomes of the initiatives. Whether community is conceptualized as neighborhood, as classroom, or as research context, well-documented findings about community–university interaction still hold. As the discourse about the purpose of higher education shifts to private benefits and economic development, we cannot rely on a continued commitment to the civic responsibility of universities. This literature review demonstrates that the civic commitment in its current form is not sufficient to address concerns raised throughout the monograph about further disenfranchisement of already marginalized groups of community residents. Advancing an engagement-as-process ethos is an important step in ameliorating those concerns about who participates in community planning and decision making.

Maintaining a Commitment to Civic Responsibility

The literature documents consistent characteristics of community–university interaction when university actors conceptualize community in specific ways. However, at many institutions, engagement is coming to be treated as a fad, something that leaders can now move beyond in pursuit of a new set of goals (Moore & Ward, 2008; O'Meara & Rice, 2005). The support of senior leaders and the commitment or interest of faculty and students cannot be taken for granted. The following recommendations suggest strategies for maintaining institutional commitment to authentic engagement with communities served by the university.

Community as Neighborhood: Institutional Partnerships.

1. *(Continually) Assess and advance institutional readiness for collaboration.* Collaborative work is "hard work and frequently messy" (Curwood, Munger, Mitchell, Mackeigan, & Farrar, 2011, p. 16). Scholars and practitioners address this by focusing on communication among diverse partners and other aspects of ongoing collaborations. Questions about context, intragroup factors, and intergroup factors could be addressed in the early stages of planning a civic engagement activity, such as "Is necessary commitment present from the institution, department, and individual faculty?"; "How will we share power, responsibility, and authority?"; and "What will collaboration look like for our group?" (Curwood et al., 2011, pp. 19–22).

2. *Plan for effective partnerships.* Administrators in search of models for effective partnerships enjoy almost an embarrassment of riches as the literature trends to superfluity in this area. What we know: the qualities of effective community–university partnerships include partnership management; group cohesion; cooperative goal setting and planning; and shared power, resources, and decision making (McNall et al., 2009). University units that support effective partnerships by pursuing a focused, outward-looking mission provide direct service and education opportunities to community partners, and research resulting in practical applications (Friedman, 2009, pp. 93–94; Maddux, Bradley, Fuller, Darnell, & Wright, 2007). The best approaches to community–university engagement include a dynamic framework involving multiple individuals with various capacities, and a clear governance model for partnerships with higher representation of community volunteers compared to university faculty (Barnes et al. 2009; Chester & Dooley, 2011).

3. *Take a systems-focused approach to changing institutional culture and behavior.* Systems thinking calls, for example, for the establishment of a university-wide structure to advance the democratic potential of community–university partnerships (Larson & McQuiston, 2012; Ostrander, 2004). Barnes et al. (2009) identify four characteristics of systemic relationships for community engagement in higher education: grounded in research partnerships, focused on capacity building for community partners, led to long-term relationships with communities, and resulted in collaborative networks within and across the community and university. These relationships must exist at multiple levels within the university to realize their potential for transforming the institution's operation.

Community as Classroom: Civic Engagement.

1. *Value and capitalize on the role of place in community–university engagement.* I have argued elsewhere that engagement is inherently place-based, and as such presents a profound opportunity for utilizing place-based pedagogies to engage students with real-world problems as a vehicle for exploring foundational knowledge in a particular discipline. One might refer to this as teaching in Pasteur's Quadrant (Stokes, 1997). This approach both extends the faculty/researcher's awareness of community issues in need of investigation, or appropriately addressed through service-learning or other civic engagement activities, and supports the preparation of civic-minded graduates (Steinberg et al., 2011) recommended in the next section.
2. *Redefine student success.* Much concern has been expressed in the last three decades about the relative health of U.S. democracy, given declining civic participation (Morse, 1989; Saltmarsh & Hartley, 2011). The potentially dire consequences of such a predicament are only further highlighted as we turn to community members to identify problems and take active roles in advancing research and community-based problem solving initiatives. When university leaders reflect upon the purpose of their institution, particularly concerning the desired outcomes of a college education, they must give thought to if and how the curricular and cocurricular experiences on

their campus prepare students to engage and plan accordingly for the development of civic-minded graduates (Bringle & Steinberg, 2010). Civic engagement "may be one of the most powerful and most effective methods for achieving civic learning outcomes" (Steinberg et al., 2011, p. 19).

3. *Recognize faculty and institutional responsibility to support student success.* Discussions of student civic engagement intersect with the broader discussion of student engagement as crucial to student success. The student engagement model, as defined by Kuh, Kinzie, Buckley, Bridges, and Hayek (2007), emphasizes the responsibility of both students and the institution for retention and graduation. Institutions have a responsibility to provide structures and programming to facilitate student engagement, and students must engage in educationally purposeful activities to realize the benefits of those activities. Immediately upon committing to prepare civic-minded graduates, institutions must attend to the structures, such as service-learning centers, and policy including those related to rewarding engaged faculty work that will further this goal.

Community as Research Context: Engaged Scholarship.

1. *Plan for engagement at each stage of the research process.* Despite the demonstrated efficacy of community-initiated research endeavors (Cook, 2008), state and federal legislative and agency attitudes and funding patterns continue to promote university-led partnerships. Ross et al. (2010) provide a useful roadmap for academic and community research partners, offering questions for consideration by each party at each stage, from the establishment of the partnership through finding funding, data collection, analysis, and dissemination, and in sustaining the partnership.

2. *Add seats at the research table.* The staff at the Center for Urban Research Learning (CURL) at Loyola University-Chicago have institutionalized a collaborative research design process that Nyden and Percy (2010) refer to as "adding seats at the research table" (p. 313). The research is initiated by representative(s) of the community organization, who present questions to be answered about the population they serve, the effectiveness of their programs, or other relevant issues facing the community that they might

address. One such project: a study to determine how programs and services offered by the Chicago Alliance to End Homelessness might need to change to address the expanded presence of older people among Chicago's homeless population (George, Krogh, Watson, & Wittner, 2008). Participation by CBO representatives varies across projects, to include all stages of the research process.

3. *Prioritize sustainability of research partnerships.* Despite being widely discussed in the public health literature, sustainability is not precisely defined. Israel et al. (2006) suggest three dimensions to be considered: relationships and commitments among the partners; "knowledge, [institutional] capacity, and values" shared among the partners; and community capacity built through the partnership (Israel et al., 2006, p. 1024). The sustainability of these programs relies in large measure on the establishment of reciprocal partnerships characterized by shared power and mutual trust (Garber, Epps, Bishop, & Chapman, 2010; Larson & McQuiston, 2012; Zandee, 2012).

Advancing Engagement-as-Process

The literature also points to three important areas of policy and practice that must be addressed to avoid further disenfranchising community members from already marginalized groups. The following recommendations offer specific strategies for advancing the critical shift from engagement as outcome to engagement as the process by which university actors interact with the community they serve.

Community Leadership for Engagement. Community deliberation must be the genesis for engagement ideas, and community leaders should drive the process of establishing collaborative relationships.

1. *Support community deliberation.* Schneekloth and Shibley (1995), together with small groups of graduate students, contributed to the restructuring of the Roanoke Neighborhood Partnership (RNP), featured in the second chapter. Acting as consultants and facilitators, the authors and their graduate students assisted residents and city leaders to design and facilitate community discussions from which ideas for restructuring the RNP emerged. This is a model that might be fruitfully applied in many other

community situations, supporting CBO leaders or groups of residents to identify problems that might be resolved through the collection and analysis of empirical data.

2. *Prioritize community leadership in research design.* Community-based participatory research projects are much more likely to lead to action when initiated by community-based organizations or government entities, rather than university researchers (Cook, 2008). Funders and other policymakers can influence the expansion of this practice by including it in requests for proposals and policy guidelines governing projects requiring or encouraging partnership.

3. *Facilitate easy access to university knowledge resources/research capacity for community-based organizations.* Community leaders face a challenge beyond identifying the issues. Universities are not intuitively designed to facilitate the interaction between community members and university personnel. A growing number of community-engaged research centers exist in the United States, providing much more direct access for representatives of CBOs to university-trained researchers (Tryon & Ross, 2012). These centers or other points of easy access are needed on many more campuses in order to realize a shift to engagement-as-process as standard operating procedure.

Faculty Rewards. Faculty can provide critical support to community processes as knowledge resources; therefore, engaged scholarship and its impact in the community must be valued in the faculty reward system.

1. *Realign the institutional economy to encourage engaged faculty work.* For more than 25 years, higher education leaders have been extolling the potential and the responsibility of higher education institutions to serve the public good. While individual faculty members are often the primary institutional actors furthering community-engaged work (O'Meara, Sandmann, Saltmarsh, & Giles, 2011), faculty at research institutions seem to find it particularly difficult to balance engaged scholarship with their institution's expectations for scholarly work. Indeed, nearly every list of barriers to engaged scholarship includes a discussion of promotion and tenure systems, faculty rewards policies, and/or administrators' attitudes toward

engagement as a key constellation of issues limiting faculty involvement in engaged scholarship and other community–university interaction across disciplines (e.g., Calleson, Jordan, & Seifer, 2005; Ellison & Eatman, 2008; Van de Ven, 2007). Institutional leaders will need to respond both at the individual level, though promotion and tenure policies, and from a systems perspective, via the institutional economy as represented in the faculty rewards system (O'Meara, 2010).

Ongoing Evaluation. Evaluation should be built into each aspect of the interaction, reflecting the university's commitment to assess the impact of the institution and its various actors on the community.

1. *Examine and report benefits of participation for communities.* The impact of community–university engagement activities on communities remains understudied and therefore underreported in the scholarship. Perhaps more troubling are the themes that Bortolin (2011) identified in her analysis of the discourse about "community" in articles appearing in the *Michigan Journal of Community Service Learning* between Spring 2008 and Spring 2010. She found that university is privileged over community, and furthermore that community is most often framed in ways that focus on how community serves the interests of the higher education institution. Prioritizing community leadership in research design for community-based research and adding seats at the research table will address the negative impact of a university-centric discourse to some extent. Beyond decentering higher education institutions in civic engagement, making changes to the research design and implementation processes should also facilitate more intentional focus on benefits to community both in the studies themselves and in the scholarship reporting on them.

2. *Use participatory approaches for process evaluation.* Stoecker et al. (2010) offer a three-part "model for producing and evaluating results" (p. 183): project design that begins with community outcomes in mind; an evaluation model to be integrated into, rather than implemented at the end of, the project; and professional development opportunities to teach engaged scholars and administrators about working from this approach. The model posits the deepening of relationships between partners over time

(pp. 190–191) and a corresponding expansion in the scope of the impact of community engagement, from individual relationships to systems-level changes. Project evaluation, they continue, should gather information about explicitly measurable or documentable goals that project coordinators can draw on to improve the project. They continue by challenging administrators: "our commitment to evaluating the success of our efforts must be as long term and community driven as our commitment to the community change process itself" (p. 191). Further, evaluation of engagement, ideally a participatory project, ought to itself be participatory (Stoecker et al., 2010). For example, Taylor and his colleagues in Buffalo have used ongoing evaluation of the Community-as-Classroom Project as an opportunity to increase and expand buy-in from teachers to participate in this voluntary initiative within their school (Taylor & McGlynn, 2009, 2010). Treating evaluation as a process rather than an event nurtures the relationship-building potential of engaging all stakeholders in evaluating the success of a particular intervention.

Moving Engagement From Outcome to Process

Community–university engagement is a powerful approach to interactions through which many important objectives can be accomplished, including strengthening communities, improving academic and civic learning outcomes for university students, and generating new knowledge through engaged faculty scholarship. To realize the broadest possible positive impact through engagement, the broadest possible representation of "the community" must be involved. How the community is framed, or understood, matters in terms of which members of that community are included in engagement initiatives, and how they participate in those initiatives.

To say that place is socially constructed implicitly opens the door for place, or the meaning associated with that place, to be changed through conscious action (Cresswell, 2004). Shifting from one way of understanding engagement to another, as this monograph encourages university actors to do, represents a powerful opportunity to change the social construction of the communities in which engagement initiatives occur. In other words, moving from instrumentalist ideas about engagement as an outcome to relational models of engagement as a process has the potential to create communities where a broader representation of the population participates in more democratic community processes.

Adopting an engagement-as-process ethos will require institutional change, but perhaps what needs to change is not so much the institution itself in a structural sense, but instead the culture of the place. Critical geographer Harvey (1996) talks about the process of valuing things, how this valuing can and does change, and to what end. That is the order of change called for here. This is not simply about creating a new community–university partnership office, or hiring someone with previous experience in a community-based organization to serve in a boundary-spanning capacity. Indeed, these are critical institutional changes, as we learn from Weerts and Sandmann (2008, 2010; Sandmann & Weerts, 2008). The more crucial change is that of campus culture, which differs considerably from the organizational culture of nonprofit/community-based organizations (Kezar, 2011). The goal here is not to blend the cultures, but instead to use what we are learning from practitioners and scholars in order to bring about more culturally competent universities, and university actors who embrace an understanding of engagement as a long-term, relationship-building endeavor.

References

Adedokun, O., & Balschweid, M. A. (2009). Are rural 4-Hers more connected to their communities than their non-4H counterparts? *Journal of Extension, 47*(1), Article 1FEA6. Retrieved from http://www.joe.org/joe/2009february/a6.php

Adler, R. P., & Goggin, J. (2005). What do we mean by "civic engagement"? *Journal of Transformative Education, 3*(3), 236–253. doi:10.1177/1541344605276792

Afshar, A. (2005). *Community-campus partnerships for economic development: Community perspectives* (Public and Community Discussion Papers No. 2005-2). Boston, MA: Federal Reserve Bank of Boston. Retrieved from http://www.bostonfed.org/commdev/pcadp/2005/pcadp0502.pdf

Alexander, F. K. (2000). The changing face of accountability: Monitoring and assessing institutional performance in higher education. *The Journal of Higher Education, 71*(4), 411–431. doi:10.2307/2649146

Allen, K. I., Dunn, C., & Zaslow, S. (2011). Ozzie and Harriet never were: A century review of family and consumer sciences and the changing American family. *Journal of Extension, 49*(3). Retrieved from http://www.joe.org/joe/2011june/comm1.php

The American Political Science Association Task Force. (1998). Civic education in the 21st century. *PS: Political Science & Politics, 31*(3), 636–637.

Anderson, J. L. (2005). Community service as learning. In A. Kezar (Ed.), *New Directions for Higher Education: No. 131. Organizational learning in higher education* (pp. 37–48). San Francisco, CA: Jossey-Bass. doi:10.1002/he.185

Anyon, Y., & Fernández, M. A. (2007). Realizing the potential of community-university partnerships. *Change: The Magazine of Higher Learning, 39*(6), 40–45. doi:10.3200/CHNG.39.6.40-45

Armony, A. C. (2004). *The dubious link: Civic engagement and democratization.* Stanford, CA: Stanford University Press.

Ash, S. L., & Clayton, P. H. (2004). The articulated learning: An approach to guided reflection and assessment. *Innovative Higher Education, 29*(2), 17–154.

Ash, S. L., Clayton, P. H., & Atkinson, M. H. (2005). Integrating reflection and assessment to capture and improve student learning. *Michigan Journal of Community Service Learning, 11*(2), 49–60.

Astin, A., & Sax, L. (1998). How undergraduates are affected by service participation. *Journal of College Student Development, 39*(3), 251–263.

Astin, A., Sax, L., & Avalos, J. (1999). Long-term effects of volunteerism during the undergraduate years. *The Review of Higher Education, 22*(2), 187–202.

Astin, A., Vogelgesang, L., Ikeda, E., & Yee, J. (2000). *How service learning affects students.* Los Angeles: Higher Education Research Institute, University of California.

Atlas, C., Korza, P., Fiscella, J., & Bacon, B. S. (2005). *Critical perspectives: Writings on art and civic dialogue.* Washington, DC: Americans for the Arts.

Austin, A. E., & McDaniels, M. (2006). Using doctoral education to prepare faculty to work within Boyer's four domains of scholarship. In J. M. Braxton (Ed.), *New Directions for Institutional Research: No. 129. Analyzing faculty work and rewards: Using Boyer's four domains of scholarship* (pp. 51–65). San Francisco, CA: Jossey-Bass. doi:10.1002/ir.171

Barker, D. W. M., & Brown, D. W. (2009). *A different kind of politics: Readings on the role of higher education in democracy.* Dayton, OH: Kettering Foundation Press.

Barnes, J. V., Altimare, E. L., Farrell, P. A., Brown, R. E., Burnett, C. R., III, Gamble, L., & Davis, J. (2009). Creating and sustaining authentic partnerships with community in a systemic model. *Journal of Higher Education Outreach and Engagement, 13*(4), 15–29.

Bartholomay, T., Chazdon, S., Marczak, M. S., & Walker, K. S. (2011). Mapping Extension's networks: Using social network analysis to explore Extension's outreach. *Journal of Extension, 49*(6), Article 6FEA9. Retrieved from http://www.joe.org/joe/2011december/a9.php

Battistoni, R. M., Longo, N. V., & Jayanandhan, S. R. (2009). Acting locally in a flat world: Global citizenship and the democratic practice of service-learning. *Journal of Higher Education Outreach and Engagement, 13*(2), 89–108.

Becher, T., & Trowler, P. (2001). *Academic tribes and territories: Intellectual inquiry and the culture of disciplines* (2nd ed.). Buckingham, UK: Open University Press.

Beling, J. (2003). Effect of service-learning on knowledge about older people and faculty teaching evaluations in a physical therapy class. *Gerontology and Geriatrics Education, 24*(1), 31–46. doi: 10.1300/J021v24n01_03

Benson, L., & Harkavy, I. (2000). Higher education's third revolution: The emergence of the democratic cosmopolitan civic university. *Cityscape: A Journal of Policy Development and Research, 5*(1), 47–58.

Benson, L., Harkavy, I., & Puckett, J. (1996). Community participatory action research as a strategy for improving universities and the social sciences: Penn's work with the West Philadelphia Improvement Corps as a case study. *Educational Policy, 10*(2), 202–222. doi:10.1177/0895904896010002005

Benson, L., Harkavy, I., & Puckett, J. (2000). An implementation revolution as a strategy for fulfilling the democratic promise of urban-community partnerships: Penn-West Philadelphia as an experiment in progress. *Nonprofit and Voluntary Sector Quarterly, 29*(1), 24–45. doi:10.1177/0899764000291003

Bergen, M. (2011, October 14). HUD secretary: Anchor institutions are the engines of city growth [Blog post]. *Forbes.* Retrieved from http://www.forbes.com/sites/markbergen/2011/10/14/hud-secretary-anchor-institutions-are-engines-of-future-city-growth/

Berger, J., & Milem, J. (2002). The impact of community service involvement in three measures of undergraduate self-concept. *Journal of Student Affairs Research and Practice, 40*(1), 85–103.

Blouin, D. D., & Perry, E. M. (2009). Whom does service learning really serve? Community-based organizations' perspectives on service learning. *Teaching Sociology, 37*(2), 120–135. doi:10.1177/0092055x0903700201

Bok, D. (1982). *Beyond the ivory tower: Social responsibilities and the modern university.* Cambridge, MA: Harvard University Press.

Bonsall, D. L., Harris, R. A., & Marczak, J. N. (2002). The community as a classroom. In M. B. Harris (Ed.), *New Directions for Student Services: No. 100. Student Affairs and External Relations* (pp. 85–96). San Francisco, CA: Jossey-Bass. doi:10.1002/ss.72

Bortolin, K. (2011). Serving ourselves: How the discourse on community engagement privileges the university over the community. *Michigan Journal of Community Service Learning, 18*(1), 49–58.

Boyce, M. (2003). Organizational learning is essential to achieving and sustaining change in higher education. *Innovative Higher Education, 28*(2), 119–136.

Boyer, E. (1990). *Scholarship reconsidered: Priorities of the professoriate.* San Francisco, CA: Jossey-Bass.

Boyer, E. (1996). The scholarship of engagement. *Journal of Public Service and Outreach, 1*(1), 11–20.

Boyte, H. (2008). *The citizen solution: How you can make a difference.* St. Paul, MN: Minnesota Historical Society Press in association with the Kettering Foundation.

Bridger, J. C., & Alter, T. R. (2006). The engaged university, community development and public scholarship. *Journal of Higher Education Outreach and Engagement, 11*(1), 163–178.

Bringle, R. G., & Hatcher, J. A. (1996). Implementing service learning in higher education. *Journal of Higher Education, 67*(2), 221–239.

Bringle, R. G., & Steinberg, K. (2010). Educating for informed community involvement. *American Journal of Community Psychology, 46*(3–4), 428–441. doi:10.1007/s10464-010-9340-y

Brown, D. M. (2001). *Pulling it together: A method for developing service-learning and community partnerships based in critical pedagogy.* Washington, DC: Corporation for National Service.

Buch, K., & Harden, S. (2011). The impact of a service-learning project on student awareness of homelessness, civic attitudes, and stereotypes toward the homeless. *Journal of Higher Education Outreach and Engagement, 15*(3), 45–61.

Bushouse, B. K. (2005). Community nonprofit organizations and service-learning: Resource constraints to building partnerships with universities. *Michigan Journal of Community Service Learning, 12*(1), 32–40.

Butin, D. W. (2003). Of what use is it? Multiple conceptualizations of service learning within education. *Teachers College Record, 105*(9), 1674–1692.

Butin, D. W. (2006). The limits of service-learning in higher education. *The Review of Higher Education, 29*(4), 473–498.

Cadwallader, M. L. (1982). A manifesto: The case for an academic counterrevolution. *Liberal Education, 68*(4), 403–420.

Cain, R. (2012). Courageous learning about race, self, community, and social action. *Adult Learning, 23*(4), 201–205. doi:10.1177/1045159512458094

Caldwell, J., & Levine, J. F. (2009). Domestic wastewater influent profiling using mitochondrial real-time PCR for source tracking animal contamination. *Journal of Microbiology Methods, 77*, 17–22.

Calleson, D. C., Jordan, C. M., & Seifer, S. D. (2005). Community-engaged scholarship: Is faculty work in communities a true academic enterprise? *Academic Medicine*, *80*(4), 317–321. doi:10.1097/00001888-200504000-00002

Cantor, J. A. (2006). Lifelong learning and the academy: The changing nature of continuing education. *ASHE Higher Education Report Series*, *32*(2). San Francisco, CA: Wiley.

Cantor, N. (2009). A new Morrill Act: Higher education anchors the "remaking of America." *The Presidency*, *12*(3), 16–22.

Carcasson, M., & Sprain, L. (2012). Deliberative democracy and adult civic education. In L. Munoz & H. S. Wrigley (Eds.), *New Directions for Adult and Continuing Education: No. 135. Adult civic engagement in adult learning* (pp. 15–23). San Francisco, CA: Jossey-Bass. doi:10.1002/ace.20022

Catlett, B. S., & Proweller, A. (2011). College students' negotiation of privilege in a community-based violence prevention project. *Michigan Journal of Community Service Learning*, *18*(1), 34–48.

Caudron, S. (2004). *Free agent learner*. Alexandria, VA: American Society for Training and Development.

Chester, A., & Dooley, E. (2011). West Virginia University's Health Sciences and Technology Academy. *Journal of Higher Education Outreach and Engagement*, *15*(3), 87–99. Retrieved from http://openjournals.libs.uga.edu/index.php/jheoe/article/view/576/463

Church, R. L., Zimmerman, D. L., Bargerstock, B. A., & Kenney, P. A. (2002/2003). Measuring scholarly outreach at Michigan State University: Definitions, challenges, tools. *Journal of Higher Education Outreach and Engagement*, *8*(1), 141–152.

Civittolo, D., & Davis, G. A. (2011). Strengthening communities through an engaged citizenry: Opportunities for extension programming. *Journal of Extension*, *49*(3). Retrieved from http://www.joe.org/joe/2011june/pdf/JOE_v49_3comm2.pdf

Cochran-Smith, M., & Lytle, S. (2009). *Inquiry as stance: Practitioner research for the next generation*. New York, NY: Teachers College Press.

Cohen, J., & Kinsey, D. F. (1994). "Doing good" and scholarship: A service-learning study. *Journalism Educator*, *48*(4), 4–14.

Colby, A., Beaumont, E., Ehrlich, T., & Corngold, J. (2007). *Educating for democracy: Preparing undergraduates for responsible political involvement*. San Francisco, CA: Jossey-Bass/The Carnegie Foundation for the Advancement of Teaching.

Conway, J., Amel, E., & Gerwein, D. (2009). Teaching and learning in the social context: A meta-analysis of service learning's effects on academic, personal, social, and citizenship outcomes. *Teaching of Psychology*, *36*(4), 233–245.

Cook, W. K. (2008). Integrating research and action: A systematic review of community-based participatory research to address health disparities in environmental and occupational health in the United States. *Journal of Epidemiology and Community Health*, *62*(8), 668–676. doi:10.1136/jech.2007.067645

Cox, D. (2010). History of the scholarship of engagement movement. In H. E. Fitzgerald, C. Burack, & S. D. Seifer (Eds.), *Handbook of engaged scholarship: contemporary landscapes, future directions: Volume I: Institutional change* (pp. 25–38). East Lansing: Michigan State University Press.

Cress, C. M., Burack, C., Giles, D. E., Jr., Elkins, J., & Stevens, M. C. (2010). *A promising connection: Increasing college access and success through civic engagement.* Boston, MA: Campus Compact.

Cresswell, T. (2004). *Place: A short introduction.* Malden, MA: Blackwell Publishing.

Cruz, N. I. (2007, March). *Reflection and response to Katrina: Engaged educators on fire with urgency, clarity, and hope.* Keynote address presented at the Gulf South Summit on Civic Engagement, New Orleans, LA.

Cruz, N. I., & Giles, D. E., Jr. (2000). Where's the community in service-learning research? *Michigan Journal of Community Service Learning, Special Issue,* 28–34.

Curwood, S. E., Munger, F., Mitchell, T., Mackeigan, M., & Farrar, A. (2011). Building effective community-university partnerships: Are universities truly ready? *Michigan Journal of Community Service Learning, 17*(2), 15–26.

D'Este, P., & Perkmann, M. (2011). Why do academics engage with industry? The entrepreneurial university and industry motivations. *Journal of Technology Transfer, 36*(3), 316–339.

Dewey, J. (1933). *How we think.* Boston, MA: Heath.

Diaz, A., & Perrault, R. (2010). Sustained dialogue and civic life: Post-college impacts. *Michigan Journal of Community Service Learning, 17*(1), 32–43.

DiPadova-Stocks, L. N. (2005). Two major concerns about service-learning: What if we don't do it? And what if we do? *Academy of Management Learning and Education, 4*(3), 345–353.

Driscoll, A. (2008). Carnegie's community engagement classification: Intents and insights. *Change, 40*(1), 38–41.

Driscoll, A., & Lynton, E. A. (1999). *Making outreach visible: A guide to documenting professional service and outreach.* Sterling, VA: Stylus Publishing.

Drummond, C. (2009, July 27). Penntrification: Mom-and-pops keep feeling the squeeze in West Philly. *Philadelphia Weekly.* Retrieved from http://www.philadelphiaweekly.com/news-and-opinion/Penntrification-51796462.html#ixzz2Vvc1FcyE

Dubb, S., & Howard, T. (2007). *Linking colleges to communities: Engaging the university for community development.* College Park: University of Maryland. Retrieved from http://www.community-wealth.org/_pdfs/news/recent-articles/07-07/report-linking.pdf

Dugan, J. (2006). Involvement and leadership: A descriptive analysis of socially responsible leadership. *Journal of College Students Development, 47*(3), 335–343.

Dzur, A. W. (2008). *Democratic professionalism: Citizen participation and the reconstruction of professional ethics, identity, and practice.* University Park, PA: Penn State Press.

Eby, J. W. (1998). *Why service-learning is bad.* Retrieved from http://www.greatlakesed.net/Resources/documents/WhyServiceLearningIsBad.pdf

Edkins, J. (2005). Ethics and practices of engagement: Intellectuals as experts. *International Relations, 19*(1), 64–69. doi:10.1177/0047117805050062

Einfeld, A., & Collins, D. (2008). The relationships between service-learning, social justice, multicultural competence, and civic engagement. *Journal of College Student Development, 49*(2), 95–109. doi:10.1353/csd.2008.0017

Ellison, J., & Eatman, T. K. (2008). *Scholarship in public: Knowledge creation and tenure policy in the engaged university.* Syracuse, NY: Imagining America. Retrieved from http://surface.syr.edu/cgi/viewcontent.cgi?article=1002&context=ia

Endres, D., & Gould, M. (2009). "I am also in the position to use my Whiteness to help them out": The communication of Whiteness in service learning. *Western Journal of Communication, 73*(4), 418–436. doi:10.1080/10570310903279083

Engberg, M., & Fox, K. (2011). Exploring the relationship between undergraduate service-learning experiences and global perspective-taking. *Journal of Student Affairs Research and Practice, 48*(1), 85–105.

Engberg, M., & Mayhew, M. (2007). The influence of first-year "success" courses on student learning and democratic outcomes. *Journal of College Student Development, 48*(3), 241–258.

Eyler, J., & Giles, D. E., Jr. (1999). *Where's the learning in service learning?* San Francisco, CA: Jossey-Bass.

Fairweather, J. S. (1996). *Faculty work and public trust: Restoring the value of teaching and public service in American academic life.* Needham Heights, MA: Longwood Division, Allyn and Bacon. Retrieved from http://www.eric.ed.gov/ERICWebPortal/detail?accno=ED393363

Fear, F. A., Rosaen, C. L., Bawden, R. J., & Foster-Fishman, P. G. (2006). *Coming to critical engagement: An auto-ethnographic exploration.* Lanham, MD: University Press of America.

Felten, P., & Clayton, P. H. (2011). Service-learning. In W. Buskist & J. E. Groccia (Eds.), *New Directions for Teaching and Learning: No. 128. Evidence-based teaching* (pp. 75–84). San Francisco, CA: Jossey-Bass.

Fettes, M., & Judson, G. (2011). Imagination and the cognitive tools of place-making. *Journal of Environmental Education, 42*(2), 123–135.

Fischer, F. (2000). *Citizens, experts, and the environment: The politics of local knowledge.* Durham, NC: Duke University Press.

Fischer, F. (2009). *Democracy and expertise: Reorienting policy inquiry.* Oxford, UK: Oxford University Press.

Flora, C. B., & Flora, J. L. (1993). Entrepreneurial social infrastructure: A necessary ingredient. *Annals of the American Academy of Political and Social Science, 529*(1), 48–58. doi:10.1177/0002716293529001005

Florida, R. (2004). *The rise of the creative class, and how it's transforming work, leisure, community and everyday life.* New York, NY: Basic Books.

Florida, R. (2005). *Cities and the creative class.* New York, NY: Routledge.

Freire, P. (1970). *Pedagogy of the oppressed* (1st ed.). New York, NY: The Seabury Book.

Friedman, D. (2009). An extraordinary partnership between Arizona State University and the City of Phoenix. *Journal of Higher Education Outreach and Engagement, 13*(3), 89–100.

Furco, A. (1996). Service-learning: A balanced approach to experiential education. In Corporation for National Service (Ed.), *Expanding boundaries: Serving and learning* (pp. 2–6). Columbia, MD: Cooperative Education Association.

Gais, T., & Wright, D. (2012). The diversity of university economic development activities and issues of impact measurement. In J. E. Lane & D. B. Johnstone (Eds.), *Universities and colleges as economic drivers: Measuring higher education's role in economic development* (pp. 31–60). Albany, NY: SUNY Press.

Galston, W. A. (2001). Political knowledge, political engagement, and civic education. *Annual Review of Political Science, 4*, 217–234.

Garber, M., Epps, W. D., Bishop, M., & Chapman, S. (2010). The archway partnership: A higher education outreach platform for community engagement. *Journal of Higher Education Outreach and Engagement, 14*(3), 69–81.

George, C., Krogh, M., Watson, D., & Wittner, J. (2008). *Homeless over 50: The graying of Chicago's homeless population* (Final Technical Report). Chicago, IL: Center for Urban Research and Learning, Loyola University.

Giles, D. E., Jr. (2010). Journey to service-learning research. In J. Keshen, B. A. Holland, & B. E. Moely (Eds.), *Research for what? Making engaged scholarship matter* (pp. 203–221). Charlotte, NC: Information Age Publishing.

Glass, C. R., Doberneck, D. M., & Schweitzer, J. H. (2011). Unpacking faculty engagement: The types of activities faculty members report as publicly engaged scholarship during promotion and tenure. *Journal of Higher Education Outreach and Engagement, 15*(1), 7–30.

Glass, C. R., & Fitzgerald, H. E. (2010). Engaged scholarship: Historical roots, contemporary challenges. In H. E. Fitzgerald, C. Burack, & S. D. Seifer (Eds.), *Handbook of engaged scholarship: Contemporary landscapes, future directions: Volume I: Institutional change* (pp. 9–24). East Lansing: Michigan State University Press.

Glassick, C. E., Huber, M. T., & Maeroff, G. I. (1997). *Scholarship assessed: Evaluation of the professoriate* (1st ed.). San Francisco, CA: Jossey-Bass.

Glassman, M., Erdem, G., & Bartholomew, M. (2012). Action research and its history as an adult education movement for social change. *Adult Education Quarterly, 63*(3), 272–288.

González, E. R., Sarmiento, C. S., Urzua, A. S., & Luévano, S. C. (2012). The grassroots and New Urbanism: A case from a southern California Latino community. *Journal of Urbanism, 5*(2–3), 219–239.

Green, A. E. (2001). "But you aren't White": Racial perceptions and service-learning. *Michigan Journal of Community Service Learning, 8*(1), 18–26.

Gruenewald, D. A. (2003). The best of both worlds: A critical pedagogy of place. *Educational Researcher, 32*(4), 3–12.

Gruenewald, D. A. (2006). Resistance, reinhabitation, and regime change. *Journal of Research in Rural Education, 21*(9). Retrieved from http://eric.ed.gov/?id=EJ745713

Hanson, J. S., & Howe, K. R. (2011). The potential for deliberative democratic civic education. *Democracy and Education, 19*(2), Article 3. Retrieved from http://democracyeducationjournal.org/home/vol19/iss2/3

Hartley, M., & Soo, D. (2009). Building democracy's university. In M. Tight, K. H. Mok, J. Huisman, & C. Morphew (Eds.), *The Routledge international handbook of higher education* (pp. 397–408). New York, NY: Taylor & Francis Group.

Harvey, D. (1993). From space to place and back again: Reflections on the condition of postmodernity. In J. Bird, B. Curtis, T. Putnam, G. Robertson, & L. Tickner (Eds.), *Mapping the futures: Local cultures, global change* (pp. 3–29). London, UK: Routledge.

Harvey, D. (1996). *Justice, nature and the geography of difference.* Malden, MA: Blackwell Publishing.

Hecht, B. (2012, January 13). Anchored in place: Creating a framework for growth [Blog post]. *The Catalyst: Ideas and Insights from Living Cities.* Retrieved from http://www.livingcities.org/blog/?id=16

Heifetz, R. A., & Laurie, D. L. (1997). The work of leadership. *Harvard Business Review, 75*(1), 124–134.

Herts, R. (2011). *From outreach to engaged place-making: Understanding public land-grant university involvement in tourism planning and development* (Doctoral dissertation). Rutgers, The State University of New Jersey, New Brunswick, New Jersey.

Hodges, R. A., & Dubb, S. (2012). *The road half traveled: University engagement at a crossroads.* East Lansing: Michigan State University Press.

Holland, B. A. (2009). Will it last? Evidence of institutionalization at Carnegie classified community engagement institutions. In L. Sandmann, C. Thornton, & A. Jaeger (Eds.), *New Directions in Higher Education: No. 147. Institutionalizing community engagement in higher education: The first wave of Carnegie classified institutions* (pp. 85–98). San Francisco, CA: Jossey-Bass.

Holland, B. A., & Gelmon, S. B. (1998). The state of the "engaged campus": What have we learned about building and sustaining university-community partnerships? *AAHE Bulletin, 51*(2), 105–108. Retrieved from http://westmont.edu /_offices/provost/documents/Curriculum/GE/Workshops/2007%20Service%20Learning %20Workshop/S-L%20Workshop-Engaged%20Campus.pdf

Holland, D., Powell, D., Eng, E., & Drew, G. (2010). Models of engaged scholarship: An interdisciplinary discussion. *Collaborative Anthropologies, 3,* 1–36.

Holsapple, M. A. (2012). Service-learning and student diversity outcomes: Existing evidence and directions for future research. *Michigan Journal of Community Service Learning, 18*(2), 5–18.

Hyman, D., Gurgevich, E., Alter, T., Ayers, J., Cash, E., Fahnline, D., … Wright, H. (2001/2002). Beyond Boyer: The UniSCOPE model of scholarship for the 21st century. *Journal of Higher Education Outreach and Engagement, 7*(1–2), 41–65.

Israel, B. A., Krieger, K., Vlahov, D., Ciscke, S., Foley, M., Fortin, P., … Tang, G. (2006). Challenges and facilitating factors in sustaining community-based participatory research partnerships: Lessons learning from the Detroit, New York City, and Seattle urban research centers. *Journal of Urban Health: Bulletin of the New York Academic of Medicine, 83*(6), 1022–1040. doi:10.1007/S11524-006-9110-1

Jacoby, B. (2006). Bottom line: Making politics matter to students. *About Campus, 11*(4), 30–32. doi:10.1002/abc.178

Jaeger, A. J., Dunstan, S., Thornton, C., Rockenbach, A. B., Gayles, J. G., Haley, K. J. (2013). Put theory into practice. *About Campus, 17*(6), 11–15.

Jaeger, A. J., & Thornton, C. H. (2005). Moving toward the market and away from public service?: Effects of resource dependency and academic capitalism. *Journal of Higher Education Outreach and Engagement, 10*(3), 53–67. Retrieved from http://openjournals.libs.uga.edu/index.php/jheoe/article/view/131/119

Jay, G. (2008). Service learning, multiculturalism, and the pedagogies of difference. *Pedagogy, 8*(2), 255–281. doi:10.1215/15314200-2007-040

Jencks, C., & Riesman, D. (1968). *The academic revolution.* Garden City, NY: Doubleday.

Johnstone, D. B. (2012). The impact of the 2008 Great Recession on college and university contributions to state and regional economic growth. In J. E. Lane & D. B. Johnstone (Eds.), *Universities and colleges as economic drivers: Measuring higher education's role in economic development* (pp. 277–294). Albany, NY: SUNY Press.

Jones, S. R., & Abes, E. S. (2004). Enduring influences of service-learning on college students' identity development. *Journal of College Student Development, 45*(2), 149–166.

Keane, J., & Allison, J. (1999). The intersection of the learning region and local and regional economic development: Analysing the role of higher education. *Regional Studies: The Journal of the Regional Studies Association, 33*(9), 896–902.

Keen, C., & Hall, K. (2008). Post-graduation service and civic outcomes for high financial need students of a multi-campus, co-curricular service-learning college program. *Journal of College and Character, 10*(2), 1–15. doi:10.2202/1940-1639.1066. Retrieved from http://www.degruyter.com/view/j/jcc.2008.10.2/jcc.2008.10.2.1066/jcc.2008.10.2.1066.xml

Keen, C., & Hall, K. (2009). Engaging with difference matters: Longitudinal student outcomes of co-curricular service-learning programs. *The Journal of Higher Education, 80*(1), 59–79.

Keith, M., & Pile, S. (1993). *Place and the politics of identity.* New York, NY: Routledge.

Kellogg Commission on the Future of State and Land-Grant Universities. (1999). *Returning to our roots: Executive summaries of the reports of the Kellogg Commission on the Future of State and Land-Grant Universities.* Washington, DC: National Association of State Universities and Land-Grant Colleges, Office of Public Affairs.

Kemmis, S., & McTaggart, R. (2005). Participatory action research: Communicative action and the public sphere. In N. Denzin & Y. S. Lincoln (Eds.), *Handbook of qualitative research* (3rd ed., pp. 559–603). Thousand Oaks, CA: Sage.

Kendall, J. (Ed.). (1990). *Combining service and learning: A resource book for community and public service* (Vols. 1–3). Raleigh, NC: National Society for Experiential Education.

Kezar, A. (2005a). Editor's notes. In A. Kezar (Ed.), *New Directions for Higher Education: No. 131. Organizational learning in higher education* (pp. 1–6). San Francisco, CA: Jossey-Bass. doi:10.1002/he.183

Kezar, A. (2005b). What campuses need to know about organizational learning and the learning organization. In A. Kezar (Ed.), *New Directions for Higher Education: No. 131. Organizational learning in higher education* (pp. 7–22). San Francisco, CA: Jossey-Bass. doi:10.1002/he.182

Kezar, A. (2011). Organizational culture and its impact on partnering between community agencies and postsecondary institutions to help low-income students attend college. *Education and Urban Society, 43*(2), 205–224.

Knapp, T., Fisher, B., & Levesque-Bristol, C. (2010). Service-learning's impact on college students' commitment to future civic engagement, self-efficacy, and social empowerment. *Journal of Community Practice, 18*(2–3), 233–251. doi:10.1080/10705422.2010.490152

Komives, S. R., Lucas, N., & McMahon, T. R. (2006). *Exploring leadership: For college students who want to make a difference* (2nd ed.). San Francisco, CA: Jossey-Bass.

Kuh, G. D., Kinzie, J., Buckley, J. A., Bridges, B. K., & Hayek, J. C. (2007). Piecing together the student success puzzle: Research, propositions, and recommendations. *ASHE Higher Education Report, 32*(5). San Francisco, CA: Jossey-Bass.

Kyle, G., & Chick, G. (2007). The social construction of a sense of place. *Leisure Sciences, 29*, 209–225. doi:10.1080/01490400701257922

Lane, J. E. (2012). Higher education and economic competitiveness. In J. E. Lane & D. B. Johnstone (Eds.), *Universities and colleges as economic drivers: Measuring higher education's role in economic development* (pp. 1–30). Albany, NY: SUNY Press.

Lane, J. E., & Johnstone, D. B. (2012). *Universities and colleges as economic drivers: Measuring higher education's role in economic development.* Albany, NY: SUNY Press.

Lankshear, C., & Knobel, M. (2004). *A handbook for teacher research.* Maidenhead, UK: Open University Press, McGraw-Hill Education.

Larson, K., & McQuiston, C. (2012). Building capacity to improve Latino health in rural North Carolina: A case study in community-university engagement. *Journal of Community Engagement and Scholarship, 5*(1), 14–23.

Lechuga, V. M., Clerc, L. N., & Howell, A. K. (2009). Power, privilege, and learning: Facilitating encountered situations to promote social justice. *Journal of College Student Development, 50*(2), 229–244.

Lee, J. (2005). Home away from home or foreign territory? How social class mediates service-learning experiences. *Journal of Student Affairs Research and Practice, 42*(3), 310–325.

Lefrançois, D., & Ethier, M.-A. (2010). Translating the ideal of deliberative democracy into democratic education: Pure utopia? *Educational Philosophy & Theory, 42*(3), 271–292.

Levine, A. (1980). *Why innovation fails: The institutionalization and termination of innovation in higher education.* New York, NY: SUNY Press.

Levine, J. F., Hargett, G., McCann, J. P., Potts, P. D., & Pierce, S. (2011). The Wilson Bay Initiative, Riverworks, and the Sturgeon City Partnership: A case study for building effective academic-community partnerships. *Journal of Higher Education Outreach and Engagement, 15*(3), 121–134.

Lewis, S., Baird, P., Evans, R. G., Ghali, W. A., Wright, C. J., Gibson, E., & Baylis, F. (2001). Dancing with the porcupine: Rules for governing the university–industry relationship. *Canadian Medical Association Journal, 165*(6), 783–785.

Link, A. N., Siegel, D. S., & Bozeman, B. (2007). An empirical analysis of the propensity of academics to engage in informal university technology transfer. *Industrial and Corporate Change, 16*(4), 641–655. doi:10.1093/icc/dtm020

Liu, G. (1996). Origins, evolution and progress: Reflections on the community service movement in American higher education. *Metropolitan Universities, 7*(1), 25–38.

Lynton, E. A., & Elman, S. E. (1987). *New priorities for the university: Meeting society's need for applied knowledge and competent individuals.* San Francisco, CA: Jossey-Bass.

Maddux, H. C., Bradley, B., Fuller, D. S., Darnell, C. Z., & Wright, B. D. (2007). Active learning, action research: A case study in community engagement, service-learning, and technology integration. *Journal of Higher Education Outreach and Engagement, 11*(3), 65–80.

Markus, G. B., Howard, J. P. F., & King, D. C. (1993). Integrating community service and classroom instruction enhances learning: Results from an experiment. *Educational Evaluation and Policy Analysis, 15*(4), 410–419.

Mathews, D. (2009). Afterword: Ships passing in the night? In D. W. M. Barker & D. W. Brown (Eds.), *A different kind of politics: Readings on the role of higher education in democracy* (pp. 93–104). Dayton, OH: Kettering Foundation Press.

Maurrasse, D. J. (2001). *Beyond the campus: How colleges and universities form partnerships with their communities* (1st ed.). New York, NY: Routledge.

Maurrasse, D. J. (2010). Standards of practice in community engagement. In H. E. Fitzgerald, C. Burack, & S. D. Seifer (Eds.), *Handbook of engaged scholarship: Contemporary landscapes, future directions: Volume II: Community-campus partnerships* (pp. 223–234). East Lansing: Michigan State University Press.

Mayhew, M. J., & Engberg, M. E. (2011). Promoting the development of civic responsibility: Infusing service-learning practices in first-year "success" courses. *Journal of College Student Development, 52*(1), 20–36.

McDowell, G. R. (2001). *Land-grant universities and extension into the 21st century: Renegotiating or abandoning a social contract.* Ames: Iowa State University Press.

McNall, M., Reed, C., Brown, R., & Allen, A. (2009). Brokering community–university engagement. *Innovative Higher Education, 33*(5), 317–331. doi:10.1007/s10755-008-9086-8

Meisel, W., & Hackett, R. (1986). *Building a movement: A resource book for students in community service.* Boston, MA: Campus Outreach Opportunity League.

Mendoza, P. (2012). The role of context in academic capitalism: The industry-friendly department case. *The Journal of Higher Education, 83*(1), 26–48. doi:10.1353/jhe.2012.0002

Miller, P. (2008). Examining the work of boundary spanning leaders in community contexts. *International Journal of Leadership in Education, 11*(4), 353–377. doi:10.1080/13603120802317875

Minkler, M. (2005). Community-based research partnerships: Challenges and opportunities. *Journal of Urban Health, 82*(Suppl 2), ii3–ii12. doi:10.1093/jurban/jti034

Minkler, M., & Wallerstein, N. (2003). *Community-based participatory research for health.* San Francisco, CA: Jossey-Bass.

Mitchell, T. D. (2008). Traditional vs. critical service-learning: Engaging the literature to differentiate two models. *Michigan Journal of Community Service Learning, 14*(2), 50–65.

Moely, B. E., Furco, A., & Reed, J. (2008). Charity and social change: The impact of individual preferences on service-learning outcomes. *Michigan Journal of Community Service Learning, 15*(1), 37–48.

Moely, B. E., McFarland, M., Miron, D., Mercer, S., & Ilustre, V. (2002). Changes in college students' attitudes and intentions for civic involvement as a function of service-learning experiences. *Michigan Journal of Community Service Learning, 9*(1), 18–26.

Mondloch, A. S. (2009). One director's voice. In R. Stoecker & E. Tryon (Eds.), *The unheard voices: Community organizations and service learning* (pp. 136–146). Philadelphia, PA: Temple University Press.

Moore, T. L. (2013). Catalyst for democracy? Outcomes and processes in community-university interaction. *Journal of Community Engagement and Scholarship, 6*(1), 70–80, 145.

Moore, T. L., & Ward, K. A. (2008). Documenting engagement: Faculty perspectives on self-representation for promotion and tenure. *Journal of Higher Education Outreach and Engagement, 12*(4), 5–28.

Moore, T. L., & Ward, K. A. (2010). Institutionalizing faculty engagement through research, teaching, and service at research universities. *Michigan Journal of Community Service Learning, 17*(1), 44–58.

Morgan, W., & Streb, M. (2001). Building citizenship: How student voice in service-learning develops civic values. *Social Science Quarterly, 82*(1), 154–169. doi:10.1111/0038-4941.00014

Morse, S. (1989). Renewing civic capacity: Preparing college students for service and citizenship. *ASHE-ERIC Higher Education Report, 18*(8). Washington, DC: The George Washington School of Education and Human Development.

Morton, K. (1995). The irony of service: Charity, project and social change in service-learning. *Michigan Journal of Community Service Learning, 2*, 19–32.

Musil, C. M. (2011). Remapping education for social responsibility: Civic, global and U.S. diversity. In J. Saltmarsh & M. Hartley (Eds.), *To serve a larger purpose: Engagement for democracy and the transformation of higher education* (pp. 238–264). Philadelphia, PA: Temple University Press.

Myers-Lipton, S. J. (1998). Effect of a comprehensive service-learning program on college students' civic responsibility. *Teaching Sociology, 26*(4), 243–258. doi:10.2307/1318766

The National Leadership Council for Liberal Education and America's Promise. (2007). College learning for the new global century. *Liberal Education, 93*(1), 36–43.

The National Task Force on Civic Learning and Democratic Engagement. (2012). *A crucible moment: College learning and democracy's future.* Washington, DC: Association of American Colleges and Universities.

Nealon, J., & Giroux, S. S. (2003). *The theory toolbox: Critical concepts for the humanities, arts and social sciences.* Lanham, MD: Rowman & Littlefield.

Netter Center. (2012). Our mission—About us. *Barbara and Edward Netter Center for Community Partnerships.* Retrieved from https://www.nettercenter.upenn.edu /about-us/our-mission

Newman, F. (1985). *Higher education and the American resurgence* [Special report]. Lawrenceville, NJ: Princeton University Press and The Carnegie Foundation. Retrieved from http://www.eric.ed.gov/ERICWebPortal/detail?accno=ED265759

Novick, S., Seider, S. C., & Huguley, J. P. (2011). Engaging college students from diverse backgrounds in community service learning. *Journal of College and Character, 12*(1), 1–8. doi:10.2202/1940-1639.1767

Nyden, P., & Percy, S. (2010). Documenting impacts: Engaged research centers and community change. In H. E. Fitzgerald, C. Burack, & S. D. Seifer (Eds.), *Handbook of engaged scholarship: Contemporary landscapes, future directions: Volume II: Community-campus partnerships* (pp. 311–332). East Lansing: Michigan State University Press.

Nye, N., & Schramm, R. (1999). *Building higher education: Community development corporation partnerships.* Rockville, MD: U.S. Department of Housing and Urban Development, Office of University Partnerships. Retrieved from http://www.eric.ed.gov/ERICWebPortal/detail?accno=ED439629

O'Brien, G., & Accardo, L. M. (1996). Metropolitan universities: Economic engine for the twenty-first century. *Journal of Public Service & Outreach, 3*(1), 16–21.

O'Brien, G., Grace, N., Williams, E., Paradise, L., & Gibbs, P. (2003). Linking academic strengths to economic development: Seven habits for effective partnership in university-based economic development. *Metropolitan University: An International Forum, 14*(1), 35–40.

O'Meara, K. A. (2002). *Scholarship unbound: Assessing service as scholarship for promotion and tenure.* New York, NY: RoutledgeFalmer.

O'Meara, K. A. (2005). Encouraging multiple forms of scholarship in faculty reward systems: Does it make a difference? *Research in Higher Education, 46*(5), 479–510.

O'Meara, K. A. (2007). Striving for what?: Exploring the pursuit of prestige. *Higher Education: Handbook of Theory and Research, 22,* 121–179.

O'Meara, K. A. (2008). Graduate education and community engagement. In C. L. Colbeck, K. A. O'Meara, & A. E. Austin (Eds.), *New Directions for Teaching and Learning: No. 113. Educating integrated professionals: Theory and practice on preparation for the professoriate* (pp. 27–42). San Francisco, CA: Jossey-Bass.

O'Meara, K. A. (2010). Rewarding multiple forms of scholarship: Promotion and tenure. In H. E. Fitzgerald, C. Burack, & S. D. Seifer (Eds.), *Handbook of engaged scholarship: Contemporary landscapes, future directions: Volume I: Institutional change* (pp. 271–294). East Lansing: Michigan State University Press.

O'Meara, K. A., & Jaeger, A. J. (2006). Preparing future faculty for community engagement: Barriers, facilitators, models, and recommendations. *Journal of Higher Education Outreach and Engagement, 11*(4), 3–26.

O'Meara, K. A., & Rice, R. E. (2005). *Faculty priorities reconsidered: Rewarding multiple forms of scholarship*. San Francisco, CA: Jossey-Bass.

O'Meara, K. A., Sandmann, L. R., Saltmarsh, J., & Giles, D. E., Jr. (2011). Studying the professional lives and work of faculty involved in community engagement. *Innovative Higher Education, 36*(2), 83–96. doi:10.1007/s10755-010-9159-3

Ostrander, S. A. (2004). Democracy, civic participation, and the university: A comparative study of civic engagement on five campuses. *Nonprofit and Voluntary Sector Quarterly, 33*(1), 74–93. doi:10.1177/0899764003260588

Pascarella, E. T., Salisbury, M. H., Martin, G. L., & Blaich, C. (2012). Some complexities in the effects of diversity experiences on orientation toward social/political activism and political views in the first year of college. *Journal of Higher Education, 83*(4), 467–498.

Pascarella, E. T., & Terenzini, P. (2005). *How college affects students: A third decade of research*. San Francisco, CA: Wiley.

Pasque, P. A. (2010). Collaborative approaches to community change. In H. E. Fitzgerald, C. Burack, & S. D. Seifer (Eds.), *Handbook of engaged scholarship: Contemporary landscapes, future directions: Volume II: Community-campus partnerships* (pp. 295–310). East Lansing: Michigan State University Press.

Perkmann, M., & Walsh, K. (2009). The two faces of collaboration: Impacts of university-industry relations on public research. *Industrial and Corporate Change, 18*(6), 1033–1065.

Perreault, G. (1997). Citizen leader: A community service option for college students. *NASPA Journal, 34*(2), 147–156.

Peters, S. J., Alter, T. R., & Schwartzbach, N. (Eds.). (2010). *Democracy and higher education: Traditions and stories of civic engagement*. East Lansing: Michigan State University Press.

Peters, S. J., Jordan, N. R., Adamek, M., & Alter, T. R. (Eds.). (2005). *Engaging campus and community: The practice of public scholarship in the state and land-grant university system*. Dayton, OH: Kettering Foundation Press.

Plater, W. M. (1995). Future work: Faculty time in the 21st century. *Change, 27*(3), 22–33.

Pounder, J. S. (2001). New leadership and university organizational effectiveness: Exploring the relationship. *Leadership and Organization Development Journal, 22*(6), 281–290.

Prigge, G. W., & Torraco, R. J. (2007). University-industry partnerships: A study of how top American research universities establish and maintain successful partnerships. *Journal of Higher Education Outreach and Engagement, 11*(2), 89–100.

Ramaley, J. A. (2000). Change as a scholarly act: Higher education research transfer to practice. In A. Kezar & P. Eckel (Eds.), *New Directions for Higher Education: No. 110. Moving beyond the gap between research and practice in higher education* (pp. 75–88). San Francisco, CA: Jossey-Bass.

Ramaley, J. A. (2002). Moving mountains: Institutional culture and transformational change. In R. M. Diamond (Ed.), *A field guide to academic leadership* (pp. 59–74). San Francisco, CA: Jossey-Bass.

Ramaley, J. A., & Holland, B. H. (2005). Modeling learning: The role of leaders. In A. Kezar (Ed.), *New Directions for Higher Education: No. 131. Organizational learning in higher education* (pp. 75–86). San Francisco, CA: Jossey-Bass. doi:10.1002/he.188

Randall, L. M., & Coakley, L. A. (2007). Applying adaptive leadership to successful change initiatives in academia. *Leadership and Organization Development, 28*(4), 325–335.

Ravitch, D. (2007). *EdSpeak: A glossary of education terms, phrases, buzzwords, and jargon.* Alexandria, VA: Association for Supervision and Curriculum Development.

Reardon, K. M. (1999). Promoting community development through empowerment planning: The East St. Louis Action Research Project. In D. Keating & N. Krumholz (Eds.), *America's poorest urban neighborhoods: Urban policy, redevelopment and planners* (pp. 124–139). Newbury Park, CA: Sage.

Reardon, K. M. (2003). Riding the rails. *Shelterforce Online, 128.* Retrieved from http://www.nhi.org/online/issues/128/ridingrails.html

Reardon, K. M., Green, R., Bates, L. K., & Kiely, R. C. (2009). Commentary: Overcoming the challenges of post-disaster planning in New Orleans: Lessons from the ACORN housing/university collaborative. *Journal of Planning Education and Research, 28*(3), 391–400. doi:10.1177/0739456x08327259

Rhoads, R. A. (1998). In the service of citizenship: A study of student involvement in community service. *Journal of Higher Education, 69*(3), 277–297.

Rhoads, R. A. (2009). Learning from students as agents of social change: Toward an emancipatory vision of the university. *Journal of Change Management, 9*(3), 309–322. doi:10.1080/14697010903125555

Rittel, H. W. J., & Webber, M. M. (1973). Dilemmas in a general theory of planning. *Policy Sciences, 4*(2), 155–169.

Robinson, J. W., & Meikle-Yaw, P. A. (2007). Building social capital and community capacity with signature projects: A case of two diverse Delta communities. *Journal of Extension, 45*(2), Article 2FEA4. Retrieved from http://www.joe.org/joe/2007april/a4.php

Rockquemore, K., & Schaffer, R. (2000). Toward a theory of engagement: A cognitive mapping of service-learning experiences. *Michigan Journal of Community Service Learning, 7*(1), 14–25.

Ross, L., Loup, A., Nelson, R., Botkin, J., Kost, R., Smith, J., Jr., & Gehlert, S. (2010). The challenges of collaboration for academic and community partners in a research partnership: Points to consider. *Journal of Empirical Research on Human Research Ethics, 5*(1), 1–16.

Rutheiser, C. (2012). Foreword. In R. A. Hodges & S. Dubb (Eds.), *The road half traveled: University engagement at a crossroads* (pp. ix–xi). East Lansing: Michigan State University Press.

Saltmarsh, J. (2005). The civic promise of service learning. *Liberal Education, 91*(2), 50–55.

Saltmarsh, J., Giles, D. E., Jr., O'Meara, K. A., Sandmann, L. R., Ward, E., & Buglione, S. (2009). The institutional home for faculty engagement: An investigation of reward policies at engaged campuses. In B. E. Moeley, S. A. Billig, & B. A. Holland (Eds.), *Creating our identities in service-learning and community engagement* (pp. 3–30). Charlotte, NC: Information Age Publishing.

Saltmarsh, J., & Hartley, M. (Eds.). (2011). *To serve a larger purpose: Engagement for democracy and the transformation of higher education.* Philadelphia, PA: Temple University Press.

Saltmarsh, J., Hartley, M., & Clayton, P. H. (2009). *Democratic engagement white paper* (Occasional Paper No. 45). Boston, MA: New England Resource Center for Higher Education. Retrieved from http://scholarworks.umb.edu/nerche_pubs/45

Saltmarsh, J., & Zlotkowski, E. (Eds.). (2011). *Higher education and democracy: Essays on service-learning and civic engagement.* Philadelphia, PA: Temple University Press.

Sandmann, L. R. (2008). Conceptualization of the scholarship of engagement in higher education: A strategic review, 1996–2006. *Journal of Higher Education Outreach and Engagement, 12*(1), 91–104.

Sandmann, L. R., Kliewer, B. W., Kim, J., & Omerikwa, A. (2010). Toward understanding reciprocity in community-university partnerships: An analysis of select theories of power. In J. Keshen, B. A. Holland, & B. E. Moely (Eds.), *Research for what? Making engaged scholarship matter* (pp. 3–23). Charlotte, NC: Information Age Publishing.

Sandmann, L. R., Moore, T. L., & Quinn, J. (2012). Center and periphery in service-learning and community engagement: A postcolonial approach. In J. A. Hatcher & R. G. Bringle (Eds.), *Understanding service-learning and community engagement: Crossing boundaries through research* (pp. 25–46). Charlotte, NC: Information Age Publishing.

Sandmann, L. R., & Weerts, D. J. (2008). Reshaping institutional boundaries to accommodate an engagement agenda. *Innovative Higher Education, 33*(3), 181–196.

Sandy, M., & Holland, B. A. (2006). Different worlds and common ground: Community partner perspectives on campus-community partnerships. *Michigan Journal of Community Service Learning, 13*(1), 30–43.

Schneekloth, L. H., & Shibley, R. G. (1995). *Placemaking: The art and practice of building communities.* New York, NY: Wiley.

Schön, D. A. (1995). Knowing-in-action: The new scholarship requires a new epistemology. *Change, 27*(6), 26–34.

Scobey, D. (2010). Across: The heterogeneity of civic education. In M. B. Smith, R. S. Nowacek, & J. L. Bernstein (Eds.), *Citizenship across the curriculum* (pp. 185–198). Bloomington: Indiana University Press.

Seider, S. C., & Hillman, A. (2011). Challenging privileged college students' othering language in community service learning. *Journal of College and Character, 12*(3), 7–14.

Seider, S. C., Huguley, J. P., & Novick, S. (2013). College students, diversity and community service learning. *Teachers College Record, 115*(3), 1–44.

Senge, P. (1990). *The fifth discipline.* New York, NY: Doubleday.

Shaffer, D., & Wright, D. J. (2010). *A new paradigm for economic development: How higher education institutions are working to revitalize their regional and state economies.* The Rockefeller Institute of Government, the State University of New York at Albany, NY. Retrieved from http://www.rockinst.org/pdf/education/2010-03-18-A_New_Paradigm.pdf

Shagoury, R., & Power, B. M. (2012). *Living the questions: A guide for teacher research* (2nd ed.). Portland, ME: Stenhouse Publishers.

Shannon, J., & Wang, T. R. (2010). A model for university–community engagement: Continuing education's role as convener. *The Journal of Continuing Higher Education, 58*(2), 108–112. doi:10.1080/07377361003661499

Sharp, J. S., Flora, J. L., & Killacky, J. (2003). Networks and fields: Corporate business leader involvement in voluntary organizations of a large nonmetropolitan city. *Journal of the Community Development Society, 34*(1), 36–56.

Skocpol, T., & Fiorina, M. P. (Eds.). (1999). *Civic engagement in American democracy*. Washington, DC: The Brookings Institution Press.

Slaughter, S., & Leslie, L. L. (1997). *Academic capitalism: Politics, policies, and the entrepreneurial university* (1st ed.). The Johns Hopkins University Press.

Slaughter, S., & Rhoades, G. (2004). *Academic capitalism and the new economy: Markets, state, and higher education*. Baltimore, MA: The Johns Hopkins University Press.

Smith, G. A. (2002). Place-based learning: Learning to be where we are. *Phi Delta Kappan, 83*(8), 584–594.

Smith, M. B., Nowacek, R. S., & Bernstein, J. L. (2010). *Citizenship across the curriculum*. Bloomington: Indiana University Press.

Sobel, D. (2004). *Place-based learning: Connecting classrooms and communities* (1st ed.). Great Barrington, MA: The Orion Society.

Sorenson, G., Emmons, K., Hunt, M. K., Barbeau, E., Goldman, R., Peterson, K., ... Berkman, L. (2003). Model for incorporating social context in health behavior interventions: Applications for cancer prevention for working-class, multiethnic populations. *Preventative Medicine, 37*(3), 188–197.

Sorenson, J., & Lawson, L. (2011). Evolution in partnership: Lessons from the East St. Louis action research project. *Action Research, 10*(2), 150–169.

Southern Regional Education Board. (1973). *Service-learning in the South: Higher education and public service, 1967–1972*. Atlanta, GA: Author.

Spellings Commission. (2006). *A test of leadership: Charting the future of U.S. higher education*. Washington, DC: U.S. Department of Education.

Stanton, T. (1987). Service learning: Groping toward a definition. *Experiential Education, 12*(1), 2–4.

Stanton, T., Giles, D. E., Jr., & Cruz, N. I. (1999). *Service-learning: A movement's pioneers reflect on its origins, practice, and future*. San Francisco, CA: Jossey-Bass.

Steinberg, K., Hatcher, J. A., & Bringle, R. G. (2011). Civic-minded graduate: A north star. *Michigan Journal of Community Service Learning, 18*(1), 19–33.

Stenhouse, V. L., & Jarrett, O. S. (2012). In the service of learning and activism: Service learning, critical pedagogy, and the problem solution project. *Teacher Education Quarterly, 39*(1), 51–76.

Stoecker, R., Beckman, M., & Min, B. H. (2010). Evaluating community impact of higher education civic engagement. In H. E. Fitzgerald, C. Burack, & S. D. Seifer (Eds.), *Handbook of engaged scholarship: Contemporary landscapes, future directions: Volume II: Community-campus partnerships* (pp. 177–196). East Lansing: Michigan State University Press.

Stoecker, R., & Tryon, E. (Eds.). (2009). *The unheard voices: Community organizations and service learning*. Philadelphia, PA: Temple University Press.

Stokes, D. E. (1997). *Pasteur's quadrant: Basic science and technological innovation*. Washington, DC: Brookings Institution Press.

Strand, K., Marullo, S., Cutforth, N., Stoecker, R., & Donohue, P. (2003). *Community-based research and higher education: Principles and practices*. San Francisco, CA: Jossey-Bass.

Sullivan, W. M. (2005). *Work and integrity: The crisis and promise of professionalism in America*. San Francisco, CA: Jossey-Bass.

Taylor, H. L., Jr. (2005, October). *Are community schools effective pathways out of poverty?* Paper presented at the National Symposium on Community Schools as Vehicles for School and Community Revitalization: Rebuilding Social Capital through Community Schools and the Role of Higher Education, Center for Urban Studies, University of Buffalo, Buffalo, NY.

Taylor, H. L., Jr., & McGlynn, L. G. (2009). The connection: Schooling, youth development, and community building—The Futures Academy case. In I. Harkavy & M. Hartley (Eds.), *New Directions for Youth Development: No. 122. Universities in partnership: Strategies for education, youth development, and community renewal* (pp. 19–40). San Francisco, CA: Jossey-Bass.

Taylor, H. L., Jr., & McGlynn, L. (2010). The "Community as Classroom Initiative": The case of the Futures Academy in Buffalo, NY. *University and Community Schools*, 8(1–2), 31–44. Retrieved from http://www.centerforurbanstudies.com /documents/publications-reports-papers/publications/community_as_classroom.pdf

Thursby, J. G., & Thursby, M. C. (2011). Has the Bayh-Dole act compromised basic research? *Research Policy*, 40(8), 1077–1083. doi:10.1016/j.respol.2011.05.009

Tierney, W. G. (1988). Organizational culture in higher education: Defining the essentials. *The Journal of Higher Education*, 59(1), 2–21.

Tripp Umbach. (2010). *University of Iowa: Economic impact report. Executive summary*. Retrieved from http://www.uiowa.edu/~impact/exec-summary/index.html

Tryon, E., & Ross, J. A. (2012). A community-university exchange project modeled after Europe's science shops. *Journal of Higher Education Outreach and Engagement*, 16(2), 197–211.

USC Rossier School of Education. (2013, February 11). *2013 USC Pullias Lecture given by SUNY Chancellor Nancy Zimpher* [Video file and transcript]. Retrieved from http://www.youtube.com/watch?v=-v6GNvGWIK8

Van de Ven, A. H. (2007). *Engaged scholarship: A guide for organizational and social research*. New York, NY: Oxford University Press.

Vidal, A., Nye, N., Walker, C., Manjarrez, C., & Romanik, C. (2002). *Lessons from the Community Outreach Partnership Center Program: Final report prepared for the U.S. Department of Housing and Urban Development*. Washington, DC: The Urban Institute.

Vogelgesang, L., & Astin, A. (2000). Comparing the effects of community service and service-learning. *Michigan Journal of Community Service Learning*, 7(1), 25–34.

Ward, K. A. (2003). Faculty service roles and the scholarship of engagement. *ASHE-ERIC Higher Education Report*, 29(5). San Francisco, CA: Jossey Bass.

Ward, K. A., & Moore, T. L. (2010). Engaged scholarship and the scholarship of engagement: Defining engagement. In H. E. Fitzgerald, C. Burack, & S. D. Seifer (Eds.), *Handbook of engaged scholarship: Contemporary landscapes, future directions: Volume I: Institutional change* (pp. 39–54). East Lansing: Michigan State University Press.

Ward, K. A., & Wolf-Wendel, L. (2000). Community-centered service learning: Moving from doing for to doing with. *American Behavioral Scientist*, 43(5), 767–780.

Warren, J. L. (2012). Does service-learning increase student learning? A meta-analysis. *Michigan Journal of Community Service Learning*, 18(2), 56–61.

Weerts, D. J., & Sandmann, L. R. (2008). Building a two-way street: Challenges and opportunities for community engagement at research universities. *The Review of Higher Education*, 32(1), 73–106.

Weerts, D. J., & Sandmann, L. R. (2010). Community engagement and boundary-spanning roles at research universities. *The Journal of Higher Education*, 81(6), 702–727.

Welsh, R., Glenna, L., Lacy, W., & Biscotti, D. (2008). Close enough but not too far: Assessing the effects of university-industry research relationships and the rise of academic capitalism. *Research Policy, 37*(10), 1854–1864.

Williams-Jones, B. (2005). Knowledge commons or economic engine—What's a university for? *Journal of Medical Ethics, 31*(5), 249–250. doi:10.1136/jme.2005.012278

Wolff, E. (2011). Recent trends in household wealth in the U.S.: Rising debt and the middle class squeeze. In J. Gonzalez (Ed.), *Economics of wealth in the 21st century* (pp. 1–41). New York, NY: Nova Science Publishers.

Worrall, L. (2007). Asking the community: A case study of community partner perspectives. *Michigan Journal of Community Service Learning, 14*(1), 5–17.

Zandee, G. (2012). Mapping a strategic plan for health: Community-based participatory research with underserved, low-income, urban neighborhoods. *Journal of Higher Education Outreach and Engagement, 16*(3), 95–98.

Zlotkowski, E. (1995). Does service-learning have a future? *Michigan Journal of Community Service Learning, 2*(1), 123–133.

Zlotkowski, E. (2001). Mapping new terrain: Service-learning across the disciplines. *Change, 33*(1), 25–33. doi:10.1080/00091380109601775

Name Index

A

Abes, E. S., 49, 50
Accardo, L. M., 6, 27
Adamek, M., 80
Adedokun, O., 24
Adler, R. P., 42
Afshar, A., 76
Alexander, F. K., 27
Allen, A., 7, 24, 33, 92
Allen, K. I., 23
Allison, J., 10
Alter, T. R., 4, 29, 31, 36, 55, 71, 80
Altimare, E. L., 92, 93
Amel, E., 46
Anderson, J. L., 34
Anyon, Y., 7, 76, 77
Ash, S. L., 47
Astin, A., 47, 48–49
Atlas, C., 70
Austin, A. E., 79
Avalos, J., 49
Ayers, J., 7, 80

B

Bacon, B. S., 70
Baird, P., 73
Balschweid, M. A., 24
Barbeau, E., 68
Bargerstock, B. A., 66
Barker, D. W. M., 4, 8, 29, 45, 55, 83
Barnes, J. V., 92, 93

Bartholomay, T., 23
Bartholomew, M., 36
Bates, L. K., 4, 8, 55
Battistoni, R. M., 47, 49
Bawden, R. J., 4, 55, 77
Baylis, F., 73
Beaumont, E., 41, 42, 58, 59
Becher, T., 89
Beckman, M., 7, 8, 9, 11, 76, 77, 78, 97, 98
Beling, J., 62
Benson, L., 25, 69
Bergen, M., 29
Berger, J., 47
Berkman, L., 68
Bernstein, J. L., 44
Biscotti, D., 73, 74
Bishop, M., 95
Blaich, C., 42
Blouin, D. D., 53
Bok, D., 3
Bonsall, D. L., 45
Bortolin, K., 9, 11, 51, 54, 97
Botkin, J., 94
Boyce, M., 90
Boyer, E., 3, 7, 46, 79, 89
Boyte, H., 45
Bozeman, B., 73
Bradley, B., 92
Bridger, J. C., 4, 29, 31, 36, 55
Bridges, B. K., 94

Moely, B. E., 49
Mondloch, A., 53
Moore, T. L., 4, 12, 14, 33, 56, 65, 66, 80, 84, 92
Morgan, W., 49
Morse, S., 63, 93
Morton, K., 54
Munger, F., 92
Musil, C. M., 43
Myers-Lipton, S. J., 59

N
Nealon, J., 9
Nelson, R., 94
Novick, S., 50, 62
Nowacek, R. S., 44
Nyden, P., 94
Nye, N., 7

O
O'Brien, G., 6, 27
O'Meara, K. A., 7, 77, 78, 79, 80, 81, 89, 91, 96, 97
Omerikwa, A., 83
Ostrander, S. A., 93

P
Paradise, L., 27
Pascarella, E. T., 42, 63
Pasque, P. A., 76, 77, 78
Percy, S., 94
Perkmann, M., 73
Perrault, R., 47, 50, 62
Perry, E. M., 53
Peters, S. J., 71, 80
Peterson, K., 68
Pierce, S., 68
Pile, S., 13
Plater, W. M., 40
Potts, P. D., 68
Pounder, J. S., 33
Powell, D., 66
Power, B. M., 62
Prigge, G. W., 24
Proweller, A., 47
Puckett, J., 25

Q
Quinn, J., 84

R
Ramaley, J. A., 33, 35
Randall, L. M., 33
Ravitch, D., 52
Reardon, K. M., 4, 8, 24, 25, 55
Reed, C., 7, 24, 33, 49, 92
Rhoades, G., 74
Rhoads, R. A., 44, 59
Rice, R. E., 7, 80, 91
Riesman, D., 65, 90
Rittel, H. W. J., 85
Robinson, J. W., 24
Rockenbach, A. B., 9
Rockquemore, K., 49
Romanik, C., 7
Rosaen, C. L., 4, 55, 77
Ross, J. A., 96
Ross, L., 94

S
Salisbury, M. H., 42
Saltmarsh, J., 8, 44, 45, 46, 51, 61, 80, 81, 83, 89, 91, 93, 96
Sandmann, L. R., 6, 7, 10, 81, 83, 84, 96, 99
Sandy, M., 7, 8, 52, 53, 54, 55, 90
Sarmiento, C. S., 70, 71, 72, 83
Sax, L., 48
Schaffer, R., 49
Schneekloth, L. H., 18, 19, 20, 31, 95
Schramm, R., 7
Schwartzbach, N., 71, 80
Schweitzer, J. H., 66
Schön, D. A., 7
Scobey, D., 48
Seider, S. C., 48, 50, 51, 62
Seifer, S. D., 96
Senge, P., 34, 35
Shaffer, D., 27, 28
Shagoury, R., 62
Shannon, J., 22
Sharp, J. S., 11

Subject Index

A
Academically based service-learning, 45–48
American Political Science Association
  Task Force, 41
Anchor institution, 17, 18, 29–32, 34
Anchor Institution Task Force, 26
Annie E. Casey Foundation, 31
Association of Public and Land-Grant
  Universities, 26, 68

B
Baton Rouge School District, 39

C
Campus leaders, 30
Campus Outreach Opportunity League
  (COOL), 44
Carnegie Foundation, 3, 14
Carnegie Foundation Community
  Engagement classification, 80
CCP. *See* Community Classroom Project
  (CCP)
Center for Community-Based Research, 68
Civic education, 48
Civic engagement, 43–55; academically
  based service-learning, 45–48;
  cocurricular, 44–45; community as
  classroom and, 93–94; community
  experiences of, 52–55; early scholarship
  on, 52; efficacy of, 55; scholarship
  related to, 48; student learning

outcomes, 48–52; teaching and learning
for, 43–52; transformative potential of,
56
"Civic mindedness," 48
Cocurricular civic engagement, 44–45
College of Public Programs, 20
Community: as classroom, 39–41, 93–94;
  as neighborhood, 92–93; as place,
  17–18; as research context, 65–66,
  94–95
Community agency directors, 53
Community-based research (CBR),
  examples of, 66–72; arts and
  humanities as public scholarship and,
  70; educational and community
  outcomes in K–12 schools, 69;
  participation processes in community
  revitalization, 70–72; prevention and
  treatment of chronic diseases, 68–69;
  water quality and wetlands restoration,
  67–68
Community Classroom Program, 69
Community Classroom Project (CCP), 69
Community deliberation, 95–96
Community development, 4
Community-engaged scholarship, 69, 75,
  79, 86–87
Community impact, in scholarship, 51
Community leadership for engagement,
  95–96
Community tourism, 20–21

intended outcomes of, 41–43; scholars and practitioners, 11

Higher education institutions, 27; changing structure of, 34; as "economic units," 28; placemaking and, 19; public good and, 42; in regional tourism, 20; role in community, 17

Higher education leaders, 6

I

Imagining America (IA), 70

Institutional change, 32–37; as scholarly act, 34–35; leadership and, 33–34; methodologies to advance, 35–37

Institutional culture, 82–88; deliberative democracy, 85–86; methodologies to explore, 86–88; postcolonial theory, 84–85

Institutional partnerships, 92–93

Institutional purpose, 55–63; critical pedagogy of place, 60–61; methodologies to transform, 61–63; place-based learning, 56–60

Institutions, act as leaders, 30

K

Kellogg Foundation, 26

L

Learning spaces, 62

M

Marga, Inc., 26

Michigan Journal of Community Service Learning, 97

N

National Task Force on Civic Learning and Democratic Engagement, 41, 42, 43

New York Times, 40

O

Osher Lifelong Learning Institute programs, 22

P

Place-based learning, 56–58; critical pedagogy and, 58–61

Placemaking, 19–26; community tourism, 20–21; community–university partnerships, 24–26; continuing education and, 21–22; higher education institutions in, 19; as three-part phenomenon, 20; university extension, 22–24

Place or location, role in engagement, 11–14; community–university interactions and, 11; conceptualizing communities, 13; for critical geographers, 12; people invest in, 13; social construction of, 13

Practitioner research, 62

Public scholarship, 80; arts and humanities as, 70; emerge from commitment to university, 72

R

REAL. See Rural Entrepreneurship though Action Learning (REAL)

RNP. See Roanoke Neighborhood Partnership (RNP)

Roanoke Neighborhood Partnership (RNP), 19, 20, 95

Rural Entrepreneurship though Action Learning (REAL), 57–58

S

SACReD. See Santa Ana Collaborative for Responsible Development (SACReD)

Santa Ana Collaborative for Responsible Development (SACReD), 71

Scholarship Assessed, 79

Scholarship Reconsidered: Priorities of the Professoriate, 79

Scholar–practitioners, 84

Service-learning, 40; academically based, 45–48; civic education, 48; course design in, 46–48; early scholarship on, 52; value of, 45–46

Spellings Commission, 42
Student learning outcomes, 48–52; impact of personal characteristics, 50–52; impact of "community service," 48; service-learning, 49–50

U

UACS. *See* University-assisted community schools (UACS)
Unheard Voices: Community Organizations and Service-Learning, The, 53
Universities, act as facilitators, 30
University-assisted community schools (UACS), 69

University extension, 22–24; contribution to placemaking, 23; issues addressed by professionals of, 23; lifelong learning opportunities, 22
University–industry collaborations, 72–76
Urban planning scholar–practitioners, 19
USC Rossier School of Education, 27

W

WEPIC. *See* West Philadelphia Improvement Corps (WEPIC)
West Philadelphia Improvement Corps (WEPIC), 25

About the Author

Tami L. Moore is an assistant professor of educational leadership and policy studies and serves as program coordinator for the Higher Education and Student Affairs program at Oklahoma State University. Her research agenda focuses broadly on the role of higher education institutions in the communities they serve, employing social and critical theory in the reading of community engagement. Her current projects explore issues related to the connection between civic engagement and postsecondary access, the work of public scholars, and interrogating social/geographic place as a participant in qualitative research.

About the ASHE Higher Education Report Series

Since 1983, the ASHE (formerly ASHE-ERIC) Higher Education Report Series has been providing researchers, scholars, and practitioners with timely and substantive information on the critical issues facing higher education. Each monograph presents a definitive analysis of a higher education problem or issue, based on a thorough synthesis of significant literature and institutional experiences. Topics range from planning to diversity and multiculturalism, to performance indicators, to curricular innovations. The mission of the Series is to link the best of higher education research and practice to inform decision making and policy. The reports connect conventional wisdom with research and are designed to help busy individuals keep up with the higher education literature. Authors are scholars and practitioners in the academic community. Each report includes an executive summary, review of the pertinent literature, descriptions of effective educational practices, and a summary of key issues to keep in mind to improve educational policies and practice.

The Series is one of the most peer reviewed in higher education. A National Advisory Board made up of ASHE members reviews proposals. A National Review Board of ASHE scholars and practitioners reviews completed manuscripts. Six monographs are published each year and they are approximately 144 pages in length. The reports are widely disseminated through Jossey-Bass and John Wiley & Sons, and they are available online to subscribing institutions through Wiley Online Library (http://wileyonlinelibrary.com).

Call for Proposals

The ASHE Higher Education Report Series is actively looking for proposals. We encourage you to contact one of the editors, Dr. Kelly Ward (kaward@wsu.edu) or Dr. Lisa Wolf-Wendel (lwolf@ku.edu), with your ideas.

Recent Titles

ASHE HIGHER EDUCATION REPORT

ORDER FORM SUBSCRIPTION AND SINGLE ISSUES

DISCOUNTED BACK ISSUES:

Use this form to receive 20% off all back issues of *ASHE Higher Education Report*.
All single issues priced at **$23.20** (normally $29.00)

TITLE	ISSUE NO.	ISBN

*Call 888-378-2537 or see mailing instructions below. When calling, mention the promotional code JBNND
to receive your discount. For a complete list of issues, please visit www.josseybass.com/go/aehe*

SUBSCRIPTIONS: (1 YEAR, 6 ISSUES)

☐ New Order   ☐ Renewal

U.S.	☐ Individual: $174	☐ Institutional: $327
Canada/Mexico	☐ Individual: $174	☐ Institutional: $387
All Others	☐ Individual: $210	☐ Institutional: $438

Call 888-378-2537 or see mailing and pricing instructions below.
Online subscriptions are available at www.onlinelibrary.wiley.com

ORDER TOTALS:

Issue / Subscription Amount: $ _____

Shipping Amount: $ _____
(for single issues only – subscription prices include shipping)

Total Amount: $ _____

SHIPPING CHARGES:

First Item $6.00
Each Add'l Item $2.00

*(No sales tax for U.S. subscriptions. Canadian residents, add GST for subscription orders. Individual rate subscriptions must
be paid by personal check or credit card. Individual rate subscriptions may not be resold as library copies.)*

BILLING & SHIPPING INFORMATION:

☐ **PAYMENT ENCLOSED:** *(U.S. check or money order only. All payments must be in U.S. dollars.)*

☐ **CREDIT CARD:** ☐ VISA   ☐ MC   ☐ AMEX

Card number _____ Exp. Date _____

Card Holder Name _____ Card Issue # _____

Signature _____ Day Phone _____

☐ **BILL ME:** *(U.S. institutional orders only. Purchase order required.)*

Purchase order # _____
          Federal Tax ID 13559302 • GST 89102-8052

Name _____

Address _____

Phone _____ E-mail _____

Copy or detach page and send to: **John Wiley & Sons, One Montgomery Street, Suite 1200,
San Francisco, CA 94104-4594**

Order Form can also be faxed to: **888-481-2665**

PROMO JBNND

Great Resources for Higher Education Professionals

Student Affairs Today

12 issues for $225 (print) / $180 (e)

Get innovative best practices for student affairs plus lawsuit summaries to keep your institution out of legal trouble. It's packed with advice on offering effective services, assessing and funding programs, and meeting legal requirements.

studentaffairstodaynewsletter.com

Campus Legal Advisor

12 issues for $210 (print) / $170 (e)

From complying with the ADA and keeping residence halls safe to protecting the privacy of student information, this monthly publication delivers proven strategies to address the tough legal issues you face on campus.

campuslegaladvisor.com

Campus Security Repo

12 issues for $210 (print) / $1

A publication that helps you effectively manage the challe in keeping your campus, stud and employees safe. From protecting students on camp after dark to interpreting the laws and regulations, *Campu Security Report* has answers you need.

campussecurityreport.com

National Teaching & Learning Forum

6 issues for $65 (print or e)

From big concepts to practical details and from cutting-edge techniques to established wisdom, NTLF is your resource for cross-disciplinary discourse on student learning. With it, you'll gain insights into learning theory, classroom management, lesson planning, scholarly publishing, team teaching, online learning, pedagogical innovation, technology, and more.

ntlf.com

Disability Compliance for Higher Education

12 issues for $230 (print) / $185 (e)

This publication combines interpretation of disab laws with practical implementation strategies to l you accommodate students and staff with disabi It offers data collection strategies, intervention m for difficult students, service review techniques, and more.

disabilitycomplianceforhighereducation.com

Dean & Provost

12 issues for $225 (print) / $180 (e)

From budgeting to faculty tenure and from distance learning to labor relations, *Dean & Provost* gives you innovative ways to manage the challenges of leading your institution. Learn how to best use limited resources, safeguard your institution from frivolous lawsuits, and more.

deanandprovost.com

Enrollment Management Report

12 issues for $230 (print) / $185 (e)

Find out which enrollment strategies are working for your colleagues, which aren't, and why. This publication gives you practical guidance on all aspects—including records, registration, recruit orientation, admissions, retention, and more.

enrollmentmanagementreport.com

WANT TO SUBSCRIBE?

Go online or call: 888.378.2537.

JB JOSSEY-B
A Wile

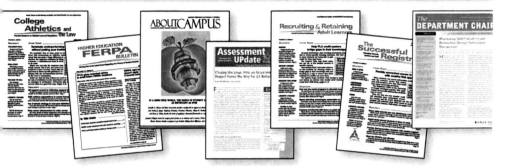

Complete Passport Renewal Appl Form DS-82
on the State Department website
call Post Office to see if it takes passport photo

CPSIA information can be obtained at www.ICGtesting.com
Printed in the USA
LVOW08s0011050216

473808LV00009B/43/P